SERVANT SELLING

SERVANT SELLING

*The Handbook for Closing More Deals
and Giving Your Customers
Exactly What They Need*

DAVE BROWN

SouthwesternBooks

Published by Southwestern Books, in partnership with Forefront Books.
Distributed by Simon & Schuster.

Library of Congress Control Number: 2023908174

Print ISBN: 978-1-63763-179-9
E-book ISBN: 978-1-63763-180-5

Cover Design by Bruce Gore, Gore Studio, Inc.
Interior Design by Bill Kersey, KerseyGraphics

This book is dedicated to the people who are the most responsible for who I am. Emmie, you are my reason for doing all I do; thank you for picking me daily. To my kids, Dawson, Cadence, and Dylan, for improving my life and being my greatest teachers; Mom (Debbie) and Dad (Rick), you are the best parents a kid could ever be blessed with; also to my siblings, Bobby, Nathan, and Alycia; all three of you enrich my life. Bobby, I would not know how to sell or have sharpened any skill in my life without you.

Together we don't lose.

Thank you, Lord, for this team you blessed me with. This book wouldn't be here without them.

CONTENTS

Part Three

COMMIT TO SUCCESS AND SERVICE

A BETTER WAY

My Own Epiphany

My epiphany came when I was twenty-two years old. I was visiting the home of Brian and Beverly Indermuhle in Smithville, Ohio, and as I presented the educational resources I was selling, an odd and uncomfortable feeling began welling up within me.

I started to feel disgusted with myself.

Ironically, I had just enjoyed connecting with some great people who were interested in purchasing learning products for their kids. But I didn't feel good about the interaction because I'd exaggerated a bit on what the products could do and the benefit they would provide. It wasn't a blatant lie or big deception—I had just stretched the truth a little. I had also answered a question from Brian and Beverly in a way that was not as forthright and factual as it should have been. Instead of being fully honest, I'd changed the subject quickly to avoid their questions so that I didn't have to fully explain my product and wouldn't lose the sale.

It was an eye-opening interaction that left me feeling lousy about myself. Even worse, I knew that my leaders and mentors at the company where I worked, Southwestern Advantage, would disapprove of what I'd done.

Why did I feel the need to stretch the truth? Because I knew this family's name and excellent reputation, and I realized that their recommendation would prove to other potential customers that the products and programs I was selling were worth purchasing.

I can still picture the kitchen table where I sat with Brian, Beverly, and their four delightful kids. I remember the feeling in the pit of my stomach. Although I believed in the products that I had shown the Indermuhles, I felt sleazy, like that old stereotype of the unscrupulous used car salesperson.

Despite my misgivings, I made the sale. And sure enough, the Indermuhles' name was gold in the community, helping me hit big sales numbers and sell more products than anyone else in the company that selling season. I received praise and recognition for how well I was doing; I won awards and shared my expertise with others in the business. I was successful.

Or was I?

I continued to wrestle with these thoughts all summer in Ohio, struggling with my identity as a salesperson and who I wanted to be in this field. When I was with others, I could ignore my concerns, but when I was alone, I felt like a self-centered fraud. I thought about other sales presentations where I had done similar things and gotten the sale but lost a piece of my integrity. It didn't happen a lot, so I convinced myself that I was justified. I told myself, "In sales, you sometimes need a little 'edge' to make the sale by exaggerating or omitting the facts, right? Everyone does it, so it's okay if I do too."

Then I remembered all the arguments I'd had growing up with my brother, Bobby, who is a year and a half younger than I am. Somehow, he always knew when I stretched the truth or conveniently left something out, just like I knew when he did. I had these same unsettled feelings after arguments with Bobby when I "won" the argument but lost a part of my integrity.

As I reflected that summer, I asked myself some questions that I still think about to this day: "Will I walk away from a sale if it is not the best thing for the person? Am I okay with losing a sale?"

After I returned home to San Antonio, Texas, at the end of the summer, I sat on my back porch, pondering these questions. Looking around the yard one beautiful day, I decided to be a servant salesperson. From that point on, my sales efforts would be focused on putting others' feelings, needs, and desires before my own.

I made this decision because I wanted to feel good about my work all the time. I wanted to sleep well at night, knowing that everyone I'd talked to that day had gotten the full truth from me no matter what the cost. To be honest, this really freaked me out. I was worried I wouldn't be successful. I wondered, *Will I stop being a top producer if I walk away from potential sales or if I don't do all I can to get the customer?* Then, clear as day, I felt like someone said to me, "Do both. Be fully honest and transparent when you're selling *and* be the best at sales."

It was the clarity I needed.

I tried to focus on servant selling throughout the rest of my twenties—and I was successful to a certain extent—but every now and then, I would struggle with the temptation to do whatever I could to make the sale instead of putting my prospects' needs and desires first. Usually, that me-focused sales approach showed up when I hadn't sold anything in a long time or when I was staring at zero sales at the beginning of the month.

It took a lot of hard work and practice, but I'm proud to say that I now consistently follow the servant-selling principles that I'll be teaching you about in this book. I have been able to help my clients succeed and to grow my own business at the same time. Servant selling is a part of who I am, and I'm blessed to be working for Southwestern Family of Companies, an organization that focuses on helping people.

Today, I'm a Founding Partner of Southwestern Consulting, a sales and leadership consulting business that helps people and companies achieve their goals. Southwestern Consulting has three divisions and more than 160 certified sales and leadership coaches around the world who use our custom workshops, scripts, and coaching curricula. For several years, we have done 20 to 25 percent growth in revenue and profits each year while being true to our principles.

My work enables me to reach thousands of people every year, as a motivational speaker, coach, and certified trainer. I help people learn how to "get over themselves" and genuinely serve their team members and customers. And I've been able to do it with the right heart and motives.

This Book Is for You

I've written this book for those of you who are seeking something different for your sales career—something more rewarding. Maybe you are already selling with integrity but want to take your career to a higher level. Or maybe you feel stuck, uncomfortable, or frustrated about your job, or you're even considering another career. If that describes you, don't give up yet, at least not until you finish this book. As you'll see, I've helped a lot of people figure out how to succeed in sales *and* feel good about doing it.

On the other hand, maybe you've enjoyed success in sales, but you still feel unsatisfied. Or maybe it *looks* like you've succeeded in sales, but your bank account tells a different story. Appearances can be deceiving, especially in the sales space where everyone wants to look confident and successful.

Whatever your reason for picking up this book, I've got good news. Servant selling is a proven strategy that works for every demographic, in every industry, even with people who know nothing about selling. How you go about selling matters a great deal. The approach, skills, and systems I'll share will be just what you need to increase your sales and enhance your job satisfaction.

In Part 1: Prepare to Serve, I'll explain the key components of servant selling and the foundations necessary to achieve success. In Part 2: Understand the Service and Sales Cycle, I'll focus on the sales skills you need to master the sales cycle. Finally, in Part 3: Commit to Success, I will show you how to create concrete systems and utilize game-changing time-management strategies to scale your success.

At the end of each chapter, I'll offer action steps you can take to become a strong servant seller and improve your results. And, of course, I'll always challenge you to reach for that next level of success. As you integrate everything you learn in this book, you will start to have greater peace of mind, forever evolving to become a salesperson who people trust and respect.

I believe that when you adopt the servant selling philosophy, it will be just the beginning for you—the beginning of greater sales, more job satisfaction, and deeper joy. If I can be a servant seller, you can too. You can be a top producer while being fully honest and caring for the needs of others.

Part One

PREPARE
TO SERVE

CHAPTER 1

A COUNTERINTUITIVE SALES SOLUTION

There's More to Selling Than Closing the Deal

Every time I run a workshop or give a talk, I ask the audience, "How would you describe salespeople?" Sadly, when I ask that question, I get some unflattering responses. Inevitably, people in the audience raise their hands and describe salespeople as selfish, manipulative, and pushy.

A survey from HubSpot[1] revealed that salespeople are perceived as the least trustworthy professionals in society. (I don't know about you, but I don't want that label on me!) Only 3 percent of respondents stated that they trust sales-people—putting us just slightly ahead of politicians on the trust scale. Ouch!

We know what the general public thinks about salespeople, but what comes to their mind when I say the word *servant*?

When I pose this question to the groups I speak to, some people shout the names of famous service-oriented figures like Mother Teresa, Gandhi, Florence Nightingale, Martin Luther King Jr., and Jesus. These people made the world a better place by making service their top priority. They cared about people. Helped people. Sacrificed for people.

Servant selling might seem counterintuitive at first because it involves words that aren't often used together: *salesperson* and *servant*. But what if you could utilize both of those words in your sales efforts? How might that change sales for you?

The process I'll walk you through in the following pages will help you live a life of significance. When you follow the principles of servant selling, your clients will feel as good as you do when you make the sale. Why? Servant selling is far more than making your quota, winning a trip, or getting a heftier commission check. All of that can and will happen as you engage the process, but as a servant seller, your intention is not just to make more money. Your top priority is to help people.

Servant selling involves . . .

> Aligning someone's needs with your product or service so there is integrity for everyone involved.
>
> Being able to sleep every night without fear of recourse or remorse based on your sales tactics that day.
>
> Basing your sales on 100 percent conviction and 0 percent on pressure and deception.
>
> Getting a yes or a no to your questions and not a maybe.
>
> Telling the truth, even if it means you could lose the sale.
>
> Knowing your product or service so well so that you don't have to make up stories about it.

On the other hand, servant selling is not . . .

Another ploy or method to close the deal.

A methodology to feel better about yourself or justify your feelings about sales.

The next fad of personal development in the sales profession.

A brand-building technique you use to promote yourself or improve your reputation.

A negotiation strategy to get what you want personally or professionally.

Something you do for just a short season of life.

As you might have guessed, servant selling isn't always easy. Most salespeople would never admit this, but it's not as easy to sell when you don't bend the truth about your products and services. It's not as easy to sell when you tell it like it is in every sales presentation and are okay if someone doesn't buy from you. It's not as easy to sell when you're focused on asking thoughtful questions so you can fully understand the needs of your prospects.

Servant selling may be challenging at times, but there is no arguing with the results this approach has produced for me, my coworkers, and the clients I coach. With servant selling, you can choose to live a life of service, integrity, and dignity—and you'll find lasting success and help countless people as a result.

A Challenge and a Promise

The sales industry involves a lot of people. According to the US Bureau of Labor Statistics, approximately 13 million Americans work in sales jobs.[2] Americans sell a wide variety of things, including homes and mortgages; goods for wholesalers and manufacturers; and services for advertising, insurance, financial services, and securities.

Talk to anyone in the sales industry, however, and you'll realize that it's time for a change. On average, people in sales positions leave their job after just eighteen months,[3] and the industry faces an annual turnover rate of 34 percent when factoring in both voluntary and involuntary turnover.[4]

Why? Sales has become increasingly difficult. According to CSO Insights, only 60 percent of salespeople are meeting their quotas.[5] In addition, salespeople have more administrative tasks than ever, spending just 34 percent of their time interacting with potential customers.[6] Technology is also a factor. While technology has given salespeople more tools than ever, such as social media and digital sales funnels, it has extended the sales process. Buyers now come to the table with more information than ever based on their own research. Salespeople today do more, earn less, and must find a way to make it all work in this ever-changing landscape.

Sales will continue to change, but fortunately, one thing will always remain the same: everything was, is, and always will be about selling. Sales is life, and life is sales. Nothing happens in this world without someone selling something, whether it is an idea, a lifestyle, a diet, a product, a restaurant, or the idea that the Dallas Cowboys are the best NFL team.

As a parent, I'm always selling my children on an idea. For example, one night at dinner, my five-year-old daughter, Cadence, didn't want to eat her peas, so I chose to sell her on the idea. I explained how healthy foods—like peas—can help our bodies heal faster and keep us strong, which was important to me since my foot was healing from surgery. I brought in testimonials from my nine-year-old son, Dawson, asking him to take a bite of peas to show Cadence how easy it was to do. We even imagined that her spoon was an airplane that "flew" the peas into her mouth. It worked! Now, one of her favorite snacks is frozen peas.

The concept about sales as a way of life applies to other relationships too. When my wife, Emmie, and I make plans for an evening out, we're each selling our own ideas of what a great night should look like. I may want to go out for Mexican food (my favorite) while she would prefer Thai food (her favorite). We each extol the virtues of our preferred restaurant. The solution usually involves a compromise of some sort—Thai food this time, Mexican next time—but the sales process is a natural part of that dynamic.

Every vision, however small or large, must be sold to someone for it to become a reality. Every dream you have depends on your ability to sell that idea, first to yourself and then to everyone who can help you achieve it. Whether you're applying to college or securing your dream job, deciding on a family vacation, or choosing where to live, it's all driven by your ability to sell yourself or your own ideas to others. As the late motivational speaker Zig Ziglar said, "Nothing gets done until somebody sells something."

An Unexpected Purpose

I never thought much about selling when I was growing up, even though my dad was a salesperson for twenty-five years. But I have always been highly competitive.

My brother, Bobby, and I usually woke up well before the sun did. My parents didn't appreciate that, so they invested in a game they knew would keep us busy for hours: Monopoly. It worked. My selling skills developed as I cut deals with Bobby in those predawn hours. We didn't restrict our deals to the game board either. We traded properties for doing chores, saying, "Okay, I'll trade you

Park Place for Marvin Gardens—and I'll also feed the dog for two days and take out the trash." Anything to get the deal done.

Even though I could "sell" my brother on a deal, I never thought I was particularly skilled at sales, and I didn't consider it as a career option. I was focused on sports. I played as many as seven sports a year while in high school. In college, I was recruited for and played basketball, soccer, tennis, and volleyball. It made for a crazy schedule, but I loved it. I pursued a Sports and Wellness Management degree (though I wasn't sure what I would do with it), and I settled for C's, enough to stay eligible to play sports.

I was capable of more, though. One semester I bet my friends that I could get all A's if I really tried. I got a 3.9 GPA. I needed a greater purpose to drive me forward, and I found it in an unexpected place. After my sophomore year of college, I checked out a job opportunity with Southwestern Advantage in Nashville, Tennessee. Southwestern Advantage specializes in training eighteen- to twenty-year-old students with no sales experience to become passionate salespeople within three months. The program has produced a wide variety of successful people like Tennessee's US Senator Marsha Blackburn, Oklahoma Governor Kevin Stitt, US Solicitor General Kenneth Starr, entrepreneur and TV personality Chip Gaines, and Boston Consulting founder Bruce Henderson.

The leaders told me most successful dealers work very long hours a week. Based on the crazy sports schedule I had been keeping for years, I thought long hours sounded normal. The experience kicked off with a weeklong sales school in Nashville. The leaders almost kept me there for a second week of training due to my poor study habits, but I told them, "Everything will be fine. Just let me go out there." I didn't say what I was thinking: "It's a *competition*. I'm gonna win."

Our group went to Upstate New York. I was in Plattsburgh, on the border of the US and Canada, 3,300 miles from my home in San Antonio. Because I hadn't paid attention all week, I hit the streets totally unprepared, driving randomly from house to house. The next day, my manager had me follow him. He taught me everything the company had tried to teach me the week before, but now it was real.

Due to sports commitments, I could only sell for ten weeks rather than the full three months, but that didn't matter to me. I set my sights on being the company's top first-year salesperson each week. After I reached my goal (and got my picture on the front page of the company newsletter), I said, "As long as I do this, I will continue to be number one."

The second week, I came in third. I wasn't happy. But the third week, I hit a company record for the number of customers sold. My shocked field leader said, "Dude, you just made $6,000 this week." That was twice what I had made being a waiter the previous summer!

I qualified for the elite President's Club and stayed at the top for the next nine weeks. I started getting calls from seasoned salespeople at Southwestern Advantage, asking me for selling insights. Then I was asked to prepare some sales-improvement ideas to share with other salespeople at the annual awards dinner that September. From that moment, I fell in love with what I was going to do for the rest of my life.

The next summer I returned as a student leader. Once again, I could only sell for ten weeks, but I still finished second, beat by someone who sold for fourteen weeks. My third summer, I surpassed the second-place person by several thousand units. I resolved to break the company record the following summer. I achieved my goal for the highest number of units ever sold—until my good friend, who I'd helped mentor, managed to sell even more units!

Over those summers, I knocked on 52,000 doors in eight states. I went on to create the audiobook *Painless Prospecting,* and a few years later, my partners and I created a start-up business called Southwestern Consulting. We started as a seminar business, selling custom sales training events before moving to one-on-one sales and leadership coaching. When we began our consulting business, I was making thirty to sixty calls a day to set up in-office meetings. My conservative estimate is that I've now made more than 260,000 prospecting calls, and my goal is to top one million. I've spoken to over 137,000 sales professionals, and as a business we have coached more than 20,000 individuals—a number that grows daily.

My wife, Emmie, and I lead and manage the Invictus Organization in Southwestern Consulting, which generates about 50 percent of our company's revenue year after year. We have the largest team in the business, with approximately twenty coaches on our direct team and another sixty-plus coaches who are led by Invictus team members.

I'll admit, I'm a very hard worker, who still puts in sixty-hour weeks occasionally. But I truly believe my sales success has been driven by my servant-selling philosophy. I've found both financial success—and peace—by helping people, and I wouldn't want to do it any other way.

Putting the Principles into Action

What's preventing you from reaching the next level in your sales career? Be specific.

How do you see yourself as a salesperson? Positive? Negative? Neutral? Do you see yourself as a servant? Why or why not?

Take the time to think about your perspective on the sales process. Is this perspective holding you back?

What good could you do if you surpassed your sales goals this year? What would selling more empower you to do with your life? What dreams do you have for making an impact in this world? Write them down.

CHAPTER 2

WIRED TO SERVE

A Heart of Servanthood Brings Success and Satisfaction

It is easy to spot servant sellers. Their servant-minded approach is an intrinsic part of them. It's who they are. They aren't faking it or putting on a show. In a room where others are jockeying for attention, they are the ones listening to someone whom others might consider unimportant.

- When faced with a problem, they look for solutions that benefit everyone.
- When something goes wrong, they take ownership.
- When things go well, they share the credit.
- They tell everyone the same story, even when it is inconvenient or difficult.
- They know that they don't have all the answers, so they seek advice from others.

- They work hard and inspire others to do the same.

One of my favorite examples of a servant salesperson is Mark Deering, a longtime friend and super-successful financial advisor with Raymond James Financial Services. I've worked with Mark for nearly ten years, and I can say with confidence that he is 100 percent focused on improving the lives of his prospects. Mark carefully studies every product he sells and works to fully understand his prospects before he meets with them. He wants to make sure his services truly meet the goal or solve the problem his prospects are trying to address. Mark listens during 95 percent of the meeting. When he's not listening, he's asking many questions and writing everything down so he can learn as much about the client as possible.

Mark takes time to think through his answers and to put himself in the other person's shoes. I've even seen him talk himself out of selling a particular product that the potential client really wanted because he knew the product better than they did, and he understood it wasn't going to fulfill the needs they had at that time. When his product *is* the right fit for the person at the time, Mark closes the deal with skill and confidence. As we'll discover, this is one of the keys to effective servant selling: once you have established that your product or service fulfills a need, you close with persistence and enthusiasm because most people need help making decisions.

When you serve potential clients with honesty and integrity, you might feel like you're conducting a customized counseling session or teaching a masterclass. Does this sound like a dream? It's possible for anyone who cares enough to do it. Ask Mark. He considers the extra effort that he dedicates to his clients to be his service to them, and it makes his job even more fulfilling.

See Yourself Clearly

How do you view yourself as a salesperson? Do you feel like you're intruding into the life of your prospect? Do you worry that you're making people uncomfortable? If so, it doesn't have to be this way.

In chapter 1, I mentioned that many people think of leaders like Mother Teresa, Gandhi, Florence Nightingale, Martin Luther King Jr., and Jesus when they hear the word *servant*. I'm not trying to compare these iconic leaders to salespeople— obviously, these leaders faced very different trials and circumstances. But we can all benefit from examining the qualities they exhibited and exploring how we might use those qualities or attributes in our own work life.

For example, these servant leaders all shared pure motives. They didn't try to create a name for themselves or simply make tons of money. They each had another, deeper purpose. If you want to serve people in your career—whether you are selling insurance, computer software, coaching services, or books— you must look beyond materialistic success. In sales, you will often encounter doubts and resistance. But when you have a greater purpose for your work, you can push through any challenge or conflict that you face.

Anyone can be a servant in their job. Since we as salespeople are often in contact with dozens of people each day, we should be able to make a huge impact. So why do we tend to see ourselves as annoying rather than helpful, service-oriented professionals? Why do we falter when we meet the slightest resistance? Why are we tempted to tell half-truths, like I did as a college student?

Let's face it: when we have quotas and commission requirements, we feel pressure to produce results. Yes, we need to produce results, and this book will help you do that. But servant selling will help you focus on the results that *really matter*.

Selling as an opportunity to serve means putting the wants, desires, and needs of your prospects before your own. It means you are honest with all the information you share about yourself and your company. Most sales books and seminars only teach a series of questions to ask or provide a basic seven-step outline to close the sale, sending the message that you win because you made more sales. Sure, those methodologies can address your concerns, feelings, and needs. The message, however, is that you should do the program so you will make more sales, not so that you will help more people.

Again, servant selling is about helping people. That is the sole focus.

My sincere hope is that the ideas presented in the following pages will inspire you and equip you to reach your full potential as a salesperson. Later in this book, I'll provide service-oriented techniques for asking questions, closing sales, generating referrals, and much more. As you read, I hope you ask yourself: "Why am I truly in the sales business? What is my motivation? Am I doing this only to make big bucks? Or is there an opportunity to make a difference in people's lives?"

Sure, you need a paycheck, but *how* you get that paycheck will determine how much you enjoy it. When you see selling as an opportunity to serve, you'll be better positioned to enjoy your real-world success.

Caring for Your Prospects

I tried to use the servant selling approach to the extent that I understood it as a young college student. I wanted to do things the right way. For instance, I loved sitting down with an entire family around a table. My aim was to bring the family together, build them up, and engage in real conversation about education. I encouraged the parents on the great job they were doing raising their kids. I told the children how important they were, and I applauded them for caring about learning. I told stories to the kids to help them think about their future. I said that if they just made a few key choices while growing up, it would affect the rest of their lives.

"That's why your parents are concerned about your education," I told them. "They want the best for you."

Everything I did was about loving the family. Because I showed genuine interest in them, they were more open-minded to what I was presenting. Genuine sincerity isn't a sales tactic.

Later, as I progressed in my career, I would call on managers of companies where I didn't understand the business and I'd still walk out with the sale, simply because I cared about the people I was talking to. For example, when we started our consulting business, I didn't know much about mortgages. I had never bought a house. Yet I was able to convince managers to let me teach their team to sell mortgages.

Despite my early efforts to be a servant seller, though, I knew I wasn't always fully serving my customers. My epiphany with Brian and Beverly gave me a good start, but it took many years of time and investment to understand what I needed to do to stay in that place. It wasn't until I fully embraced the servant-selling approach that I began to experience both real selling success and deeper fulfillment. It happened because I became focused on truly serving people rather than just figuring out how I could connect with them to sell more. Instead of thinking of how I could sell more to meet *my* needs, I wanted to meet *their* needs with what I had to offer.

The Servant Selling Ethos

At Southwestern Consulting, we have a document titled "Servant Selling Ethos" that details what we mean by this concept. It begins this way:

> *Servant Selling is not a self-help philosophy;*
> *it's a help-others philosophy. We believe*
> *that joy, satisfaction, and significance come*
> *not from accumulating and acquiring for*
> *ourselves but by serving and supporting*
> *others to achieve their goals in life.*

Joy. Satisfaction. Significance. Who doesn't want that? When I finally learned how to sell this way—consistently—I not only enjoyed greater sales results, but I also felt more deeply fulfilled in work and life. And it has changed everything.

Now I feel content in my career choice. I don't feel like a fraud who is talking others into things they don't want. I believe strongly that sales is a prestigious profession that has lifted me and many others to unprecedented heights.

In fact, servant selling has helped me improve every relationship in my life. Even though the hardest place to practice these servant philosophies is at home with my wife and kids, I try every day to put their needs ahead of my own. When I practice these principles, everyone in our house is more considerate, happy, and peaceful.

In addition, I have grown spiritually by practicing servant selling principles. My favorite spiritual leader and teacher, the apostle Paul, said it best in my favorite book, the Bible. He wrote, "Do nothing out of selfish ambition or vain conceit. Rather, in humility value others above yourselves" (Philippians 2:3). To me, this statement nails the concept of servant selling.

As servant salespeople, we should look primarily to the interests of others. This is not natural for me; it's hard for me to put others' interests before my own. But through prayer, meditation, and coaching, I'm getting closer to this ideal way of living. I'll never perfect it, of course, but I have embraced this daily challenge to do better and be better.

You might have heard it said, "To sell is to serve." But what does it mean to truly serve people? When you are a servant seller, you love your customers. You love yourself. You love what you do. Sure, you probably don't love every minute of it, but you learn ways to remind yourself of why you do what you do. That's what sales is all about—loving people.

I love the message of servant selling because it aligns so well with what I read in the Scriptures. Jesus defined what it means to serve others. He told his disciples, "Love one another. As I have loved you, so you must love one another" (John 13:34). Jesus wanted to show others how much he loved them. As a result, his focus on serving others created connections with people, enabling him to make a significant impact on the world—both then and now.

You don't have to share my beliefs to recognize the value of Jesus's call to serve the people around us. In fact, many other spiritual leaders and great thinkers have emphasized the importance of loving people and putting others first. Everyone can benefit from the principles of servant selling.

Servant selling begins with having a servant's mindset. It's not about me but about how *I* can serve *you*. When you begin every day, every call, and every conversation with that perspective, it changes everything.

Here's what having a heart of service helps you do:

Overcome fear. When you focus on helping others, you sell "by accident." Your job becomes being helpful, valuable, and useful to as many people as you can reach. Think about that the next time you feel reluctant to call a potential client. Could it be because you're not focused on the opportunity to serve?

Subdue pride. Humility is the highest discipline. Ironically, it cultivates confidence, giving you a humble boldness in your selling. The next time you feel insecure or arrogant, you should assess whether you are focusing on service.

Create joy. There's nothing like the joy of watching someone you've helped succeed. If you don't have a heart to serve, you shouldn't be allowed to sell. If you don't feel joy in your work, maybe it's because you're not focused on serving.

Sustain motivation. You don't need to be relentless in your pursuit of success. Instead, be relentless in your pursuit of service. When you do this, you'll move from doing more so you can have more to serving more so you can do more good. This will naturally provide you with more. If you have a poor work ethic, it may be because you're not focused on serving!

Inspire greatness. Servant sellers focus on giving everyone a premier welcome so that they feel great. Insist on overdelivering and adding a finishing touch to convey how important each of your clients is to you. Your focus on service will inspire you to be great and will encourage others to do the same. If you feel complacent, it may be because you're not focused on serving.

Servants in Action

We've talked a lot about what servant selling is and is not. But what does it look like in action? One of our coaching clients, Lizzie Bishop of Heffernan Insurance Brokers in Petaluma, California, is a servant salesperson through and through. She is an executive vice president with Heffernan, a $100 million company, and she is in charge of training all new brokers. She also sits on Heffernan's board of directors. Over the years (more than a decade now) of working with us, Lizzie has not only absorbed but also practiced every single servant-selling principle we have taught her.

From our first phone call, it was easy to see she had a heart for helping others through her work. Lizzie wanted to help more clients and prospects, and she believed in the servant selling principles I had introduced to her, so she asked me to come train her people in her office. That initial meeting went so well that Lizzie and her team attended a conference to learn more.

Lizzie has learned and integrated many things from us over the years, but one of her favorite servant selling techniques and principles includes using names and success stories. This gives her credibility as a salesperson and ultimately makes her clients feel more comfortable. Lizzie also studies various approaches and closes, catering to each person's personality and needs so she can honor her prospects. She doesn't call on anyone without learning a little bit about them. Rather than push her own agenda, she honors her clients by selling the way they like to buy.

By using these principles and others, Lizzie is now one of the top executives in the insurance field.

Serving Through Good Times and Bad

Life can be hard. Sales can be tough sometimes. But having a servant's attitude changes everything. Angie Moss is another one of my favorite real-life examples of a servant seller. She has taken a servant's approach throughout her career, even during some tough times in her life.

Angie discovered she had cancer shortly after going through a divorce. After surgery, she recovered and remarried. Her new husband suggested she might be good at selling mortgages, and after a lot of learning, juggling childcare, and making calls at odd hours, she realized he was right. She was great at it.

For years, Angie's mortgage selling business thrived, and her income kept doubling. She approached her mortgage business as a consultant and servant to her potential prospects. She asked tons of questions and never pushed anyone through the process without knowing that her product was the best fit for their needs. In fact, she walked away from potential sales because she didn't feel right about getting people into a mortgage they couldn't afford. Because of her honesty and care, Angie received many referrals and developed a reputation as someone who could always be trusted in the industry.

Then came the real estate crash of 2008. Angie struggled to find the best way forward. She recalled how she had enjoyed having a coach to help her, and she became certified as a coach herself. Angie wasn't sure about becoming a coach full time, though. She was concerned she wouldn't be able to find a company where people saw sales in the same way she did.

On her first call with someone from our consulting team, she presumed the call would be a short one and said so.

"Why don't you tell me about how you define selling?" our team asked her.

"I define selling as service," Angie replied.

The line was silent for several seconds.

"That is interesting because we have long tradition of defining it the same way."

With that, Angie had found a new home.

Angie began building her new sales coaching business, quickly rising to be one of our most successful coaches. When Angie coaches someone new, she tells them they must commit to being a servant salesperson. Otherwise, she won't work with them. Angie also created an internal class for Southwestern Consulting called Elevate Mortgage, which helps people with no experience in the mortgage business to get started. Almost all her graduates have gone on to prosper in the mortgage business because of her knowledge of the industry and her commitment to teaching the servant-selling principles.

I hope the ideas presented in this chapter—and especially the stories I've shared—have demonstrated a powerful principle: a servant's heart leads to success. Even more than financial success in sales and business, however, an attitude of service leads to satisfaction and fulfillment in all of life.

Putting the Principles into Action

Check your motivation. What drives your desire to succeed in sales? What problem are you uniquely positioned to solve? Take a few moments to reflect on ways you make people's lives better by sharing your solution (product or service). Write them down.

Think about a time someone has served you tremendously well. Note what elements of that sales experience could be translated to your own servant selling process.

Read a biography or watch a documentary about a great servant leader who inspires you. Two of my favorite books are Ron Chernow's *Washington: A Life,* a portrait of our country's first president, and William Manchester's *The Last Lion,* a biography on the life of Winston Churchill. Pay attention to how these servant leaders continuously served others and at the same time advanced causes they were passionate about.

CHAPTER 3

THE POWER OF PERSISTENCE

In the Face of No, Press On

Parenting has taught me many unexpected lessons. Once our children got to an age when they could pay attention long enough to be read to, my wife, Emmie, and I started acquiring great books to share with them.

There was one particular book that I was really excited about. My parents read this book to me almost every night from the time I was three years old until I was six. When I began to read it to my kids, I fell in love with the book all over again.

See how quickly you can recognize it:

"I could not, would not, on a boat. I will not, will not, with a goat."

Sound familiar yet?

"I will not eat them in the rain. I will not eat them on a train."

I'll bet you're nodding now.

"I do not like them here or there. I do not like them anywhere! I do not like green eggs and ham! I do not like them, Sam-I-Am."

That's right. I'm referring to *Green Eggs and Ham,* by Dr. Seuss. I had nearly forgotten it, but when I started reading it again to my children, my fascination with this book returned.

Although it's a children's book, *Green Eggs and Ham* contains wisdom for people of all ages. In fact, it's probably my favorite book when it comes to understanding the secrets to sales success. It dramatically shaped my sales approach from a young age, though I didn't realize that until years later.

The entire book is about the character Sam-I-Am asking his prospect to "buy" his invitation to eat green eggs and ham. But the tall, fluffy prospect insists there's no way he'll ever try it. He's not interested. Not a chance.

How many times do you think Sam-I-Am asks his towering prospect to try green eggs and ham? *Thirty times!* And every time he asks, except for the final time, he hears, "No!" The prospect answers sometimes softly, sometimes so loudly the force nearly blows Sam-I-Am backward. But two things never change for Sam-I-Am. For one thing, he never stops smiling. Even when dark arrows are coming out of his prospect's mouth to illustrate shouting, Sam-I-Am's smile never leaves his face. Each no rolls off his back. No matter the force of rejection, he keeps smiling as if he knows something his prospect doesn't.

Another thing that never changes is his refusal to quit. No matter how many nos he gets, Sam-I-Am never stops asking for his client to at least try green eggs and ham. In fact, how many times do you think Sam-I-Am hears no before he finally gets a yes?

When I ask this question to live audiences, most people think Sam-I-Am is rebuffed twenty-nine or thirty times, because he asks thirty times. But it took a lot more than thirty refusals for Sam-I-Am to make the sale. Sam-I-Am gets an emphatic *no* seventy-five times before his prospect finally says yes and tries green eggs and ham.

And the prospect loves them! Just like Sam-I-Am knew he would.

I mention this whimsical book because persistence is a key piece of servant selling. Servant sellers follow up because we want to establish that we care about our prospects. We want the best for them, so we persist in offering a product or service that we know will help.

If you can relate to Sam-I-Am's pain and feel like there's no way you would make it through that rejection still smiling, that means you're normal! However, once you have established that your prospect has a need, and your product or service will meet that need, you can be as persistent as Sam-I-Am. As I've said before, people need help making decisions that are good for them.

Let's be honest; most salespeople would not respond to the challenge the way Sam-I-Am does. After the first no, we might not be smiling anymore. A lot of us wouldn't follow up again. We would take the rejection personally and start looking for somewhere to hide.

If normal sales results and relationships are what you're looking for, then what you're doing now may work for you. But if you're serious about reaching your potential in sales and helping people, then you should embrace Sam-I-Am's key to servant selling and recognize the power of persistence.

You Get to Choose

Now I'm the one trying to encourage my kids to pick *Green Eggs and Ham* for bedtime stories every night. I do all the voices, fun accents, and sound effects to bring it to life for them because I want them to really "get it" at a young age. I want them to form the habits necessary for success in sales—and in life—so they can build skills in the years to come.

Your success as a servant salesperson depends on the habits you form. Habits are like the pistons in the engine of a car. When properly fueled and oiled, those habits will keep you firing on all cylinders. If you don't have a well-maintained engine, though, the best fuel in the world won't get you to your destination. Neither will the priciest tires, nor will being the best-trained driver. You need your engine revving at maximum horsepower so you can put all of it together—skills, motivation, and systems—to succeed in sales.

Persistence is a learned quality. It's not a trait you're either born with or not. You can learn persistence as a habit that fuels your sales energy and strategy.

Do you want to work on persistence? There's only one way to do it. You need to go out and get rejected. In fact, the best salespeople teach themselves to accept and embrace rejection.

What's Your "No Goal"?

When I speak at live training events, I often invite three volunteers from the audience to join me on stage. After a little get-to-know-you session, I present them with a challenge. I give each of them thirty pennies. Every penny is a little different. Some are shiny and some are not. Some are old, some are new.

Then I challenge them to get me to "buy" as many as they can in ninety seconds. Almost without fail, they begin by describing how awesome a particular penny is, how shiny it is, or why the year on that penny was such a good year. Some people don't even ask me to buy because they're so busy trying to sell me on a feature of that penny. Some try to get me to imagine what I could buy with a penny. Others try to establish rapport with me and then go for a *yes*. In ninety seconds, they usually make about three or four serious attempts to make the sale. And I never buy one. I'm nice about it, and we have fun, but I never say yes.

After each person tries to sell me the pennies, we change roles and I take a turn. I ask one of them to be the buyer. Then I do my best Sam-I-Am imitation:

"Do you wanna buy this one?" I ask.

They reply, "No."

"Do you wanna buy this one?"

"No."

I persist, "Do you wanna buy this one?"

"No."

I keep going: "Do you wanna buy this one?"

"No."

By about the tenth rapid-fire ask, I can tell they're starting to think about giving in. By the twentieth ask, they're almost there. Sometime before I get to thirty, I usually get them to say yes at least once or twice before they say no the rest of the time. But I *do* get a yes. And that's 100 percent more than what they got from me.

Why? There's only one difference. I persisted, repeatedly, when I heard no.

I kept asking.

Persistence is where success begins. Is this how you, as a servant salesperson, should go about selling? Just asking people to buy with rapid-fire questions? Of course not. There needs to be a greater purpose—such as helping people—behind your persistence, or your persistence will just be noise.

Most salespeople shut down when they hear no instead of seeing it as a signal to step up. But everyone will hear no during their career, right? If you're new to sales, you might hear more nos than a sales veteran. (Maybe.) But you can set a goal for how many nos you will hear each day. Rather than setting a goal for how many closes you'll make or sales you'll get, persist until you hit your No Goal. Setting a No Goal helps make it more of a game or challenge as you adopt a new habit of persistence. You may not be able to control how many times you hear yes, but you can decide how many times you'll hear no—and keep moving forward.

This technique got me through the early days of our company when we were selling decision-makers on participating in our seminars. I was making so many calls a day that it was hard. But I set a No Goal of twenty-seven every day. I had to hear no twenty-seven times before I would call it a day. I counted every time the receptionist did not pick up my call or I didn't get in touch with the decision-maker. "Well, they told me no for the day," I figured. On average, it took me about forty-two calls to hit my No Goal. I remember pushing myself at 5:30 p.m. some days to make one more call to get to twenty-seven nos. Sometimes that call turned into an appointment, and I had to make *another* call to get my final no for the day.

When you have a No Goal, you cannot help but see as many people as possible, which is a big component of servant selling. When you see more people, you can serve more people. And when you are not emotionally dependent on getting a yes (or a sale), you are free to continue calling or knocking—with a great attitude.

Having a No Goal also helps you to realize that *no* is not personal. Your prospect isn't rejecting you when he or she says no. In fact, that person is giving you what you need to meet your goal. Do you need to improve your skills so that you hear yes more often? Absolutely. But the best skills won't matter at all if you don't first commit to persisting in the face of rejection.

Remember Sam-I-Am's example. Hearing no is just part of the process of developing persistence. Has a salesperson ever died from hearing the word *no*? Not likely. And hearing no is the only way you'll ever get more of the yes responses you really want.

I'm going to encourage you to take the No Goal a step further by applying a strategy I always use when I'm turned down, and it's called Praying for Nos. When someone rejects you or turns you away with a "not interested" or "that's not for me," you can shoot up a quick prayer and thank the Lord or the Universe for bringing that person to your path today.

This isn't formal or complicated; it's a simple sentiment. You can say something like, "Thanks, God, for putting this person in my life and allowing me to connect with them today." It's just a quick prayer expressing gratitude. By using this opportunity to refocus your thinking, you'll be better able to stay positive and serve the people around you.

The Secret Sales Success Equation

I've studied prospecting—the act of developing new clients—for decades now. In my experience, this simple equation captures how living the servant selling approach leads to sales success. It goes like this:

$$2Q \longrightarrow 2E = 8R$$

Q stands for quantity. Whatever you're selling, and however many doors you're knocking on or calls you're making, you should do twice the quantity of anyone else. When you do twice the activity, something incredibly important happens. You get twice the experience, the E in the equation. Getting that amount of additional experience bends the learning curve and can only lead to you getting better—fast. The result, the *R*, is usually eight times the normal closing rate.

I've seen it in my own sales experience, even going back to my college days. When I started selling educational systems, my supervisors said, "You just need to show your products to thirty families a day."

To do that, I worked eighty-five hours a week. I didn't have exceptional experience or skills. I wasn't the sharpest tool in the shed. But I knew I could work hard and not quit. I saw fifty-two families every single day when I was selling, and I made more than $18,000 in three months as a 19-year-old just getting started. By the fourth summer, I added skills to my habit of persistence, broke the company record, and made $106,000. Unfortunately, as a college kid, all of that was gone by October. But the results were real.

Now that you know the meaning of the terms, here again is the Secret Sales Success equation:

$$2Q(\text{Quantity}) \longrightarrow 2E(\text{Experience}) = 8R(\text{Results})$$

I've seen the $2Q \longrightarrow 2E = 8R$ equation work with sales rookies and veterans alike when they engage with persistent enthusiasm. For example, one of my coaching clients, Jon Milonas, is in commercial real estate sales. Jon is a senior vice president with CBRE in Chicago and has been with the firm for many years. He does two times the business development activity of anyone else in his group and has literally quadrupled his income since I began coaching him to apply this approach.

Jon understands that prospecting (he calls it business development) is how he serves the world. He has come to love the grind of it because he is able to help more people with their problems and needs. He loves finding the right commercial space for his clients and wants to make sure all the details—the square footage, location, and price—work for his client. What a great example of a servant salesperson! His leaders and business partners respect his constant effort to live out this equation.

This equation reinforces the fact that sales is a numbers game. You are freed up to succeed when you follow this simple formula. This is how you make prospecting painless and how you make selling a service. When you call on twice the number of people, you get twice the experience, and you multiply your results. You grow in less time, more effectively. The other benefit is that when you expect to hear no, you can push through the rejection and keep prospecting until you find the right people to help.

When we forget about the numbers game, we often start complaining about the leads we don't have and the things that aren't working in our lives. When you get into that head space, remember that sales is simple: the more people you see, the more products and services you will sell. And when you sell more, you serve more.

Top producers don't have any magic or secret powers. Sure, they've developed a skill set because they are committed to getting twice the experience. But they also know how to take rejection, embrace it, and persist through it. That's why one of my favorite mantras is this: when you're struggling to sell, the answer lies behind the next door.

We all stumble and fall, but that doesn't mean we stop trying to walk. If you'd taken that approach as a toddler, you'd still be crawling around on your hands and knees. You didn't let a little bump or even a painful fall stop you. You kept trying until you had mastered the walking process. In the same way, be persistent. Your product or service is going to help people!

Pleasantly and Playfully Persistent

I saw persistence in action when I visited my good friend Toby a few years ago. He and his wife have five children, including a daughter named Stella. Stella was two-and-a-half years old when I came for this visit. What a ball of energy! From the moment I got there, she started talking . . . and talking. She was one of those kids who doesn't stop. Immediately, she started trying to get my attention: "Dave! Dave! Dave!"

Her mom told her, "Call him Mr. Brown."

"Okay," Stella said. "Mr. Brown, can I show you my room? Mr. Brown, come over here! Mr. Brown, let's play this game!"

She whisked me away on a twenty-minute tour of her house. I saw her parents' room. I saw her room. I saw her toys. I saw how she played with her toys.

Her mom finally told me, "She just started doing this a couple months ago. Dave, you're going to have to ignore her because she'll do it nonstop for the next three or four hours. We won't be able to eat dinner or talk. So be nice about it, but ignore her."

"Okay," I thought. "That makes it easy." I politely broke off the tour and tried to ignore her.

As we sat down to dinner, though, Stella persisted. "Excuse me, Mr. Brown? Mr. Brown? Excuse me. Excuse me, Mr. Brown? Mr. Brown? Excuse me." I started counting how many times she said, "Excuse me, Mr. Brown" during dinner. It had to be fifty times.

After dinner, I heard her say, "Mom, at dinner tonight, Mr. Brown wasn't very conversational. Ugh!" Then she looked at me to make sure I was listening.

"Wow," I told her dad as we went into the living room, "*conversational* is a big word for a two-year-old!"

He and I sat on the couch, catching up on life, when Stella ran to the doorway between the kitchen and living room, where she knew I could hear her. She never stopped trying to hold my attention and engage me in conversation!

Every time I think of that story, I remember to stay persistent. Servant salespeople know to stay pleasantly and playfully persistent to get their prospect's attention, just like Stella was working to get mine.

Why Don't We Persist?

If persistence is such a foundational habit and so critical to sales success, why do we struggle to do it? For one thing, we fail to realize persistence is a way of life. It's not something we can just do occasionally and continue to grow.

The reality is that if we don't persist, we'll feel comfortable giving up. At the time of this writing, I'm wearing a protective boot on one foot. I had corrective surgery to address an old sports injury and had to be off my foot completely for several weeks. Now that it is healing, my doctor tells me I need to use my foot. According to the orthopedic physicians, the sooner I start applying pressure, the better my foot will heal. If I stay off it for too long, it will heal incorrectly and be worse than before. It needs the pressure to grow correctly.

That's how it is for all of life, isn't it? When kids struggle with math, we don't tell them to quit if they get a problem wrong. We expect them to persist and improve. If they struggle to read or to write, we tell them they will get better with practice. Persistence is a process we must embrace if we're going to succeed at anything—especially selling.

Persistence is all about seeing something through to the end. It is why, for most of my professional life, I have had the poem "Invictus" posted where I can read it every single day. William Ernest Henley wrote it in the late 1800s:

> Out of the night that covers me,
>   Black as the Pit from pole to pole,
> I thank whatever gods may be
>   For my unconquerable soul.
>
> In the fell clutch of circumstance
>   I have not winced nor cried aloud.
> Under the bludgeonings of chance
>   My head is bloody, but unbowed.
>
> Beyond this place of wrath and tears
>   Looms but the Horror of the shade,
> And yet the menace of the years
>   Finds, and shall find, me unafraid.
>
> It matters not how strait the gate,
>   How charged with punishments the scroll,
> I am the master of my fate:
>   I am the captain of my soul.

I love this poem so much that it inspired the name of the organization Emmie and I lead within Southwestern Consulting: Invictus. Every day this poem inspires me to persist in the face of whatever adversity comes my way, to put each no in perspective. If you want to be a successful servant salesperson, begin with persistence.

Putting the Principles into Action

What's your No Goal? How many nos will you aim to get each day or each week? Write this number down. Then find someone who will hold you accountable and share your No Goal with them. Explain why you picked that number and why this goal is so important to you.

Write down your favorite poem, mantra, or quote about persistence and hang it somewhere you can see it daily. You might also think of a person who is a great example of persistence and hang a picture of him or her where you can see it every day.

Think of someone who initially said no to you many times but ended up buying from you. How were you able to help? What did you say? How did you persist? Write that story down so you can go back to it when you're struggling with rejection.

CHAPTER 4

ENGAGE WITH ENTHUSIASM

Bring Your Energy and Eagerness Every Day

Frank Bettger had just started his career as a professional baseball player in 1907 making $175 per month when he was unceremoniously demoted to the minors by his manager. When Frank asked why, the manager said, "Whatever you do after you leave here, for heaven's sake, wake yourself up and put some life and enthusiasm into your work!"

Finding himself suddenly earning only $25 per month in the new league, Frank didn't feel very enthusiastic, but he made the critical decision to act enthusiastic. Here's how he described the change he chose to make:

> I made up my mind to establish the reputation of being the most enthusiastic ballplayer they'd ever seen. . . . From the minute I appeared on the field, I acted

like a man electrified. I acted as though I were live with a million batteries. I threw the ball around the diamond so fast and so hard that it almost knocked our infielders' hands apart.

Within ten days, Bettger's enthusiasm took him from $25 a month to $185 a month—an increase of 700 percent (and even more money than he was making before he was demoted)! Could he throw a ball better? Catch or hit better? Not a bit! Enthusiasm alone did it, nothing but enthusiasm.[7]

Like Frank's story shows, it's easy to lose enthusiasm, even when you're doing something as cool as playing professional baseball. But enthusiasm is key. Nothing in life is fun without enthusiasm. It's like a secret weapon. Enthusiasm gives you motivation, joy, clarity, and energy.

Servant selling and enthusiasm are forever connected like a train on tracks. One doesn't work properly without the other. If you lack enthusiasm when you are selling, it's probably because you've lost sight of helping people through your products or services. Without enthusiasm, your best will rank among average.

In fact, I'd go so far as to say that your energy level—the outward expression of your enthusiasm—itself is a choice. Certainly, there are biological exceptions, and some people have limited energy because of underlying health conditions. I'm not talking about a lack of physical energy due to physical limitations, though. I'm referring to a lack of enthusiasm that comes from losing motivation. For example, maybe your flight lands at 3:00 a.m. and you've got to be up at 7:00 a.m. for a keynote or sales presentation—it's "go time!" If you know your body can do it, then choose to bring the energy. Choose enthusiasm, and confidence will follow.

This goes for everything from parenting to relationships. Whatever activities you're involved in, if you bring enthusiasm, you will find success. People will want to be around you. Enthusiasm is contagious. It's similar to laughter in its ability to spread from one person to the next. When one child begins giggling in a classroom, what happens? A few others join in, and before you know it, there's an entire room full of kids laughing hysterically.

Think of the best-performing salesperson you know. Are they enthusiastic about what they do? I would bet that they are the best because they find joy in helping others with their needs—enthusiastically.

Jump-start Your Enthusiasm

How do you jump-start your enthusiasm? Like everything else in life, it takes focus, thought, and practice. There is no better place to practice enthusiasm than during the sales process. When you're selling, you're probably saying something similar to each prospect (by way of a talk track or script). Naturally, after saying the same things over and over, you can get bored with your script . . . unless you practice enthusiasm. To drum up enthusiasm, remind yourself of why you are selling in the first place—why you love the products or the services you sell or all the people you have been able to help. You might be giving your presentation for the hundredth time that day, but the prospect in front of you is hearing it for the first time. Bring the energy. After all, you're helping people!

When I sold educational systems, I tried to bring enthusiasm every day. To save time going from house to house, sometimes I would cut across lawns and jump bushes between yards. How many times do you think this college athlete carrying a huge box of books tried jumping a four-foot bush and didn't make it over? Plenty! Imagine forty pounds of educational products spread all over the lawn. It was a mess, but I had fun and enjoyed it.

When homeowners saw me spill my load, they came out to help me. I was always ready with a smile and a hearty, "Thank you! Oh, yeah, do you have a place we can sit down inside? Great!"

You must choose to be enthusiastic, or you will fail as a salesperson and leader. The good news is that when you force yourself to *act* enthusiastic, you *become* enthusiastic.

Enthusiasm is not a natural habit for most people. It certainly isn't for me. Sometimes I get into a city late at night and need to be up early the next morning for speaking and training. When I wake up in a new city, I don't just naturally jump out of bed smiling and ready to engage. I have to force myself to focus on the people I'll be serving. I imagine their faces. I practice positive self-talk. When I'm walking into the venue, I put a little pep in my step. I seek out people to talk to, and I shake their hands. Because I choose to be enthusiastic, I become enthusiastic.

I prove this point when I ask my audiences to engage in an activity at live events. I put people in pairs and ask one person to say, "This year is going to be the best year of my life." Then the other person responds with the same statement, but with greater enthusiasm. They say this back and forth, their enthusiasm increasing every time. After a couple of minutes, people are often yelling at the top of their lungs.

When I ask them how they feel, they all say, "Great!" Even if some of them didn't start the exercise with much energy, the increased volume and animation quickly works its magic. The participants chose to be more enthusiastic. And so can you.

Every Monday when you head into the office, every time you pick up the phone, every time you knock on a door or make a video call, you can choose to be enthusiastic about your work and the people you serve. You get to choose how you talk to your friends or family members about your sales job.

I see this in my own children. Dawson, Cadence, and Dylan are still young, but they're looking forward to the day they get to go to work. They think it's the coolest thing in the world. They're already thinking of sales success. Whether it's their dog-treat business outside the dog park on a Saturday or selling Tennessee Titans bracelets at the stadium, the kids have come up with genius ideas. And they can't wait to do more, because they are mirroring the enthusiasm they see in Emmie and me when we discuss our work.

Thermostat or Thermometer?

A lot of people think, "My circumstances dictate my enthusiasm." I disagree. That kind of thinking just makes you a victim of your environment! Think of enthusiasm as a thermostat versus a thermometer. A thermometer indicates what the temperature is in the room—it doesn't change anything. But a thermostat sets the temperature, which is what I do when I choose to bring energy and joy to a room.

Recently, I was speaking to the insurance agents at Bankers Life & Casualty Office in Winston-Salem, North Carolina. Jeff Kee, a longtime coaching client of Southwestern Consulting, runs the office at Bankers Life. He believes in the servant selling principles we teach because they have changed his life.

Jeff invited me into his office to teach these principles to his people and sign up those who were ready for our coaching program. To be honest, I was not excited about the meeting. Most of these agents were new to the industry and not making much money yet, and Jeff didn't have any budget to financially support the ones who wanted to sign up.

I booked my plane ticket from Nashville to Charlotte reluctantly, because I thought I wouldn't sell anything and that it would be a waste of my time. I even called Jeff and told him what I was thinking. What a selfish attitude! Jeff quickly reminded me of why I was selling in the first place—to help people. He said, "You don't have to come, but some of these people could use what you teach, and that in itself should be enough for you show up."

He was right. Even though I didn't feel excited at first, I chose to focus on the people and their needs, expecting nothing in return. This led to one of the most enthusiastic presentations I had given in years. We signed up four people for coaching, and they have already seen incredible results.

When you bring enthusiasm to everything you say, you sound a lot more confident—and when you're confident, you sell more. I firmly believe that the ability to bring enthusiasm to any situation starts with the words we choose, and not just the words we speak to others. The words you say to yourself carry immeasurable weight. Study after study shows that the words you use contribute to the reality you create.

If you're harnessing enthusiasm in a positive way, you might tell yourself:

"I cannot wait to help this person today."

"I'm a servant salesperson. I love serving people."

"Work is going to be so much fun."

"I cannot wait to see who's on the other side of this door or hear who picks up the phone."

"It's going to be beautiful, exactly the way it's supposed to be."

These are great examples of how self-talk can fuel enthusiasm. Obviously, you must combine enthusiasm with action, but when you do, the results will follow.

Avoid These Words

A lot of times, however, self-talk can be negative. In my experience, there are three words people use more than any others during negative self-talk. These three words hold people back. They're the biggest barriers to success in sales.

See if they feel familiar to you:

Can't

I hear people say this downer of a word all the time: "I can't do it." It's even more powerful—and destructive—when it's spoken to somebody else: "What are you thinking? You can't do that!" The word *can't* is extreme. When you say you can't do something, you'll never do it. After all, why would you even try if you can't? But you absolutely can.

Always

Sure, *always* can be a positive word. For example, "I'm always on time." Or "I always try to do the right thing." But it can be deadly if you use it in a negative way. I often hear people say things like, "I always mess it up," "I always get rejected when I call," or "Every time I talk to someone, I always get shut down."

When you say those things, what are you saying about your future?

Once I was at a bowling alley with friends, playing in a lane next to serious bowlers with wristbands and their own shoes and balls. About halfway through our game, I noticed theirs was ending and how close their teams' scores were.

One woman was preparing to knock down the two remaining pins, which would lead her team to victory. Many of us looked on with anticipation. She released the ball and missed one of the pins, and the other team cheered. The woman dropped her head. As she walked past me, I heard her mutter to herself, "D---it, Cindy, you always screw up when it matters!" My heart hurt to hear her say that. What a sad view of herself.

Many people are like Cindy, using the word *always* in a negative way. Don't tell yourself that you're always going to fail! It's not true, so don't use that word negatively.

Never

The word *never* is toxic. I've heard people say it so many times: "I'm never going to do that." "I'll never succeed." "I'll never close that sale." The more you use the word *never*, the more you slip away from being the best you can be. Don't let this word tank your enthusiasm. Avoid it at all costs.

I've noticed that the words *can't, always,* and *never* literally rank in that order for how often they show up in our sales coaching conversations. But look at the first letter of each word. Can't. Always. Never. That's right: CAN. You *can* bring enthusiasm every day to every call, every visit, and every interaction. When you choose positive self-talk, you can—and will—help the people you interact with every day.

WYDFLI!

Success comes from doing the things you don't want to do at the time. When you procrastinate or cut corners to avoid a task, you're only hurting yourself. Not doing certain things will cost you—in experience, in clients, in confidence, and in sales.

When I feel an urge to coast, here's what I say: "WYDFLI!" (Pronounced *WID-fly*.) In fact, I yell it: "WYDFLI!" We all yell it at the office: "WYDFLI!" "WYDFLI!" I even have a friend, Martine Cao, who tattooed it on his leg because he wanted to be reminded forever: WYDFLI!

WYDFLI! stands for When You Don't Feel Like It!

During those times when you don't feel like doing some-thing—when you don't want to make the next call, knock on the next door, practice your presentation, or research a prospect—yell it out and get to it!

When you make enthusiasm a habit, it changes who you are. With enthusiasm, you'll develop the persistence that you need to succeed at anything in life—especially sales, where it's easy to put off what you know you need to do.

The concept of WYDFLI enables you to serve your customers in the best way possible, because you're engaging with them and exploring all the ways you can help! WYDFLI will improve everything from your career to your relationships:

Don't want to pick up the phone? WYDFLI!

Don't want to work out today? WYDFLI!

Don't feel like eating right? WYDFLI!

Don't want to compliment your spouse? WYDFLI!

Don't feel like helping your kids with schoolwork? WYDFLI!

It works on everything when you identify it, call it out, and choose to engage with persistence and enthusiasm.

The bottom line is this: selling is an emotional process. My colleagues and I subscribe to the old saying that selling is a transference of emotion. That is so true. Sometimes the first person you need to sell is *you*. Sell yourself on engaging with persistence and enthusiasm, even when you don't feel like it (WYDFLI!), and watch your results dramatically improve!

Train Yourself to Be Enthusiastic

If you've read this chapter and decided you're just not an enthu-siastic person, allow me to persuade you that you are! Anyone who is intent on serving other people can be enthusiastic. Here are three ways to increase your enthusiasm:

Practice in a low-risk environment. If you're playing with your kids, bring the energy. If you're watching the game with your friends, bring the energy. If you're working in the yard, bring the energy. Practice jump-starting your enthusiasm in safe places with safe people, and you'll find it easier to do during sales calls.

Smile as big as you can in your next sales presentation for as long as you can. By doing this, you will increase your energy level. I do it all the time when I need to increase my enthusiasm, and it works. And when I'm excited about what I'm selling, the people I'm talking to get excited too!

Integrate high-fives into your sales presentations. This may seem like an unusual tip, but take it from someone who has given high-fives in 99 percent of all the sales situations he has been in: high-fives bring up the energy level. Really! Rarely is the other person going to leave you hanging, and each time you engage with someone, you will increase the level of enthusiasm in the presentation.

Remember, your goal is to communicate your solution in a way that is not only respectful and helpful but also enthusiastic. You are in sales because you truly believe your product or service will help people, so show your enthusiasm! Don't hold back.

Putting the Principles into Action

How healthy is your self-talk? What are you saying to yourself right now?

What do you want this year to look like? Finish these three sentences:

This year, I am . . .

This year, I can . . .

This year, I will . . .

Pay attention to the things you'd rather ignore. Why do you feel reluctant when you're prospecting, driving to a sales call, or asking for a referral? Don't push away those feelings. Become more present about the things you don't want to do, and then *just do them.* (And remember to shout, "WYDFLI!")

Next time you don't want to prospect, think about how you might be able to encourage that person. Say out loud, "What good things might happen if I reach out to Juan from my insurance company, or contact the people on Allison's list of referrals? How could my services or products make their lives better?"

Talk to the top producer down the hall. Ask what they do to maintain energy and enthusiasm, even when it's not naturally in high supply. Then follow their example.

CHAPTER 5

THE VALUE OF VISION

Servant Sellers Know Their* Why *and Plan to Fulfill It

My freshman season playing volleyball at Trinity International University (TIU) was one of the best examples I have experienced of how to cast a vision.

Lance Schrader was a young head coach, but he did not lack vision. At training camp the month before our season started, he called us all national champions. Coach Schrader had played volleyball all four years not long before at TIU and had never gotten a shot at the national championship. He told us that because he never got his shot playing for the championship, he was going to win it now as the coach and that we were the team that was going to make it happen.

Whenever we didn't want to run or perform endless drills, Coach Schrader would ask us if we thought that national champions did these drills over and over. He would always answer his own question, saying, "Look, you're doing it, and you are national champions, so the answer is yes. Get on board and keep working!"

When we lacked effort on a play in practice, he would shout, "This is not who we are!" He would mimic our halfhearted work in a melodramatic and joking manner. Then he would tell us we were champions and act out what he wanted to see from us when we were doing the drills. It was pure programming of our minds so we could execute the team's vision.

After a while, something started to happen. Players began calling each other out on habits or effort that did not portray a champion, on and off the court. It was fascinating. I was a freshman going on blind faith, so I was fully on board with Coach Schrader.

The first half of the season was a disaster. We lost 75 percent of the matches we played. It was embarrassing at times, but Coach Schrader never departed from his vision. He continued to call us champions and urged us to keep calling each other champions. Then in the second half of the season, the magic started to happen. We got our lineups right and started playing almost flawlessly. We won every conference game, beating some of the biggest schools in the nation.

We won the national championship handily.

Was this an accident? No, not to Coach Schrader and not to us players. We won because of the vision the coach had cast in front of us and reminded us of daily. We were national champions long before we ever put that banner up in our gym— which still hangs there today.

As I write this, some of those feelings are coming back to me, from the dismal start to the season, to how we worked tirelessly to improve, to how we became a well-oiled unit, to the last play that clinched the victory, to our celebration in the locker room that night. I played the libero position (defensive specialist) my freshman year, and during that last play when we needed the final point to win, I passed the ball to the setter and said out loud, "Champions!" Our middle hitter, Dennis Arensen (my college roommate), answered, "Yep!" As the ball was set right to Dennis, he hit it powerfully onto the court.

On paper, we were not the best team in the nation, but we believed in ourselves—wholeheartedly—thanks to Coach Lance Schrader. He got his championship because he first convinced himself it was possible and then helped convince us players. To this day, we are all thankful for Coach Schrader's extraordinary vision.

Years later, I drew upon that championship experience when my best friends and I started Southwestern Consulting. My business partners and I understood how essential it is to cast a vision and believe in it. Initially, we experienced a big gap between our dreams and our reality. Although we envisioned having a large team one day, at the time we had only a handful of key members.

We had a long way to go and faced many big challenges ahead, but we had vision. For example, we envisioned having a fully functioning operations department. In the early years, it consisted of just one person, but we made it our goal to grow this vital department. Within five years, it became a full operations department that we nicknamed "Special Ops" because of how excellent the team is at their work. We now have a crew of talented people who support us as coaches and trainers, managing all the details and obstacles involved with accounting, marketing, payroll, and customer service.

Vision is essential for anyone who wants to move toward greatness. Vision energizes you, guides you, and propels you forward. No matter where you are right now in your journey as a servant seller, you can cultivate a vision for the future that motivates you to succeed. And you can harness the power of that vision to set achievable goals that keep you on track.

Seeing Your Vision

Your vision is your dream. It's the big picture, the 30,000-foot view of what you want your life to look like five, ten, twenty, even thirty years from now.

Some salespeople build their vision on getting what they personally want from the sales profession and their prospects, without necessarily striving to serve their clients. In contrast, servant salespeople build their vision on helping others achieve their goals through what they sell. They understand that they will get what they want if they help their prospects get what *they* want.

How does this work, practically speaking? Many of our coaching clients work in the insurance industry. Instead of just training them to exceed their goals and make more money, we remind our insurance clients of their vision to help people. They are giving people the protection needed if a tornado touches down or an elderly parent requires long-term care services.

See the difference?

Vision and goals work in tandem to propel you forward, but they are different. Goals function as the tools to help you reverse-engineer your vision. Goals are the day-to-day, week-to-week, month-to-month short-term benchmarks you set to move you closer to a bigger vision. (In fact, goals are so important that I've dedicated an entire chapter to the topic.)

I recommend that everyone create a vision board to bring their vision to life and keep it in the forefront of their mind. A vision board is either a physical or virtual space where you can post inspiring pictures of people, places, and experiences that motivate you. Your vision board can include inspiring quotes or anything that will help you think big about the future. I suggest you create a vision board or update yours if you already have one. This is one of the first things we do with all our coaching clients.

A vision board is nothing new; many people have leveraged this popular tool. In fact, a study by TD Bank revealed that at least one in five small business owners used some form of a vision board when they started their business. Of those who did use a vision board, 76 percent reported that they achieved what they had envisioned![8]

Having a vision board encourages you to be motivated, active, and disciplined. It is a powerful external reminder of the internal vision you have for yourself as a servant seller. Having a crystal-clear vision will help you make the sacrifices needed today to turn your vision into reality.

Maybe you've never created a vision board before and are thinking, "Sounds great, Dave. But how do I get started, and what do I include on it?" The whole point of the board is to include things that inspire *you.*

At the time of this writing, I drive a 2005 Honda Accord. It's not fancy, but it gets the job done. I'm not really a fancy-car kind of guy. But I have leveraged an image of a car on my vision board to dream on a bigger scale. A few months ago, I came across a picture of a car where every piece of metal—right down to the bolts and screws—was 24-karat gold. It was a $3.2 million BMW owned by a sheikh in Abu Dhabi, and it was beautiful! I put it on my vision board, but not because I want that car. Honestly, I don't. It simply inspires me because it represents big thinking.

It's one thing to create a traditional vision board, but how do you make one that incorporates servant selling? I include quotes about serving others, pictures of people who are incredible servants, and testimonials from people whom I've helped. For example, I have added statements from people who told me, "You changed my life" and "Thanks for helping me to get the house of my dreams." By including these quotes, pictures, and testimonials, I become driven to help more people.

Over the last ten years I have made five vision boards, and I've seen some themes develop. For example, some of the consistent pieces on my vision boards include pictures of my family having incredible experiences all over the world. Each vision board has had a different picture of a beautiful winery on it because I love wine and will have a winery outside Nashville in a couple of years. I have also posted the names of each business I do private equity placements with because I love investing money in hungry entrepreneurs who have great ideas. I've included pictures of me with our Invictus Organization members in some of the coolest places in the world, as well as many pictures of our entire company at Southwestern Consulting, which continues to get bigger every year. And then I have pictures of my closest friends beside a quote by Jim McEachern: "Spend more time with less people." And of course, I do have some fun dreams for myself on there as well, like my goal to fly privately one day, but I also include nonprofits I support, people who inspire me, and encouraging Scripture.

You should put things on your vision board that you want to acquire as well as things that stretch you and excite you to think, "Wouldn't it be cool if . . . ?" Fill your vision board with images, inspiring quotations, and relationship-oriented reminders. Use it to project a future version of yourself that will motivate you as a servant seller.

What's Your Why?

Before you start cutting out images from magazines and gluing pictures on paper, you need to have a firm grasp on your *why*. Your *why* really comes prior to your vision, because your *why* should shape your vision. (As I mentioned earlier, your vision then determines your goals.)

Your unique *why* will tap into the root reasons you sell or do anything in the first place. As a servant seller, you are focused on what's best for other people. You are envisioning how you can bless the world through your work and life. Your vision gets built on what you're going to contribute to the world, not just what you're going to get. I'm not saying you shouldn't dream of driving the latest Mercedes or owning a vacation cottage on Cape Cod. Not at all. But you should also ask yourself, how much do you want to give? How many people do you want to impact? How many lives do you want to change? And what images might you see in your life if you achieve those goals? If you're still not sure what motivates you, ask yourself what your reason is for showing up to work each day.

My *why* is to help people believe in themselves more and to help them servant sell more. My *why* has become so interconnected with our company's *why* that it's hard to separate the two. Southwestern Consulting states, "The reason we exist is to help people achieve their goals in life." Over the years, I've noticed that when our partners at Southwestern Consulting take the time to dream together, our visions usually align closely because we all share the same *why*.

Over the years, my *why* has changed. At first my *why* was to win no matter what. I wanted to be successful, to know what it felt like to be number one. I'm a little chagrined to admit that my first vision board was almost completely an accumulation of pictures of possessions I wanted, as well as a few quotes about being successful and some images of piles of money. I was young and obsessed with having cooler stuff than the next person. Ugh! I still have that vision board (buried in the back of the closet) to remind myself of how much my values and vision have changed.

As I embraced the servant selling mindset, my *why* evolved to coaching others to enjoy that success. Now, I literally tell the people I coach, "I want you to be successful. That's why I'm bringing you here. I want you to have the kind of life that I have." Truth be told, I'm no longer as fulfilled when I accomplish things personally. But I feel crazy fulfilled when I get to celebrate wins by my coaching clients. My vision board today looks much different from the first one I did.

Here are some ideas for creating or updating your vision board:

Set aside uninterrupted time. Reflect on your servant selling *why.* Write down your answers, focusing on how serving others—including clients, managers, coworkers, and friends—will help you discover your *why.* (For more on finding your *why,* see the questions listed in the next section.)

Gather inspiring pictures from magazines or online. Choose pictures that align with your servant selling vision. These images should immediately prompt you to say, "Yes! That is what I want for my life!" Select a picture based on the way it makes you feel rather than a picture that is a literal representation of your vision.

Arrange the pictures on a poster board or, for the technologically savvy, arrange the digital images using an image editor.

Add service-oriented motivational words or phrases that reflect how you want to feel or what you want to accomplish through serving others. For example, one of my affirmations is,

"I am a servant to all, especially with my family; I always look for ways to help everyone around me daily." (For more information about affirmations, see chapter 14.)

Finalize your vision board. If you've created your vision board on the computer, send it to a local printer and have it printed on large, thick-stock paper. For handmade vision boards, secure pictures using tape, glue, or pins.

Put your vision board in a prominent place. To stay focused on your vision, make sure you can view your vision board every day. Find a space in your home or office where you can look at it and reflect on it regularly.

How to Find Your Why

At Southwestern Consulting, we have come up with a list of questions to help our clients figure out what motivates them. Knowing what motivates you will help inform your vision. We call this list "10 'Whats' to Find Your Servant Selling 'Why.'"

1. What energizes you about your work as a salesperson?
2. What would you want clients and colleagues to say about you when they know you're not listening?
3. What type of work in service to others would you like to do each day?
4. What would your perfect day look like in terms of how you spent your time?
5. What do you want to give back to the world? Who do you need on your team or in your life to help you fulfill this?
6. What ways are you uniquely gifted and skilled to serve others?
7. What is one change you can make to begin serving others more fully?

8. What do you want to be known for?
9. What are the things you believe in most?
10. What people do you want to spend most of your time with? How do you plan on blessing them as you do life together?

As a servant seller, it is so important to take the time to figure out your *why* and what your service-minded vision is. I'll say it again: deciding to be a servant salesperson is deciding to take the path of *more* resistance. When difficult times come, it's critical for you to be able to fall back on a really strong *why* that will keep you focused on others.

I've always believed that we are created for camaraderie. Anyone who believes they can do things on their own is really missing the best part of life—relationships. A salesperson who is self-focused will have a mediocre and self-centered career, at best. I'd rather have a vision to help people and get excited at the opportunity to bless others by putting them first each day. I hope you do the same.

Putting the Principles into Action

Create your own vision board. Review the process in this chapter. Then jump in and bring your vision to life. Keep your vision board updated and in a prominent place.

Rewrite your vision to be one that is focused on putting others' needs first.

Choose a word of the year to serve as your focus. Reflect, visualize, jot down words that come to mind, and then refine the list until you hit on the word that most speaks to you. In the past I've used the words *empathy, connection, wisdom,* and *kindness.* Your word might be a relationship quality you want to strengthen in your personal life or an idea that simply inspires you. Then, when you're setting your goals, you can decide if they are in alignment with your word of the year, which represents your vision.

Part Two

UNDERSTAND THE SERVICE AND SALES CYCLE

CHAPTER 6

PRE-APPROACH: DO YOUR HOMEWORK

If You Care, You Prepare

During my second summer selling books with Southwestern Advantage, I knocked on the door of an older woman who told me she had no children. She didn't need the educational systems I was offering.

Since I was learning to focus on serving others (rather than just trying to be number one), I wasn't disappointed or upset to hear that our books weren't a good fit for the woman. We had a friendly chat, and I asked if she could help me with my neighborhood map to save me time and so I wouldn't disturb anyone who was not a viable prospect. It was always helpful to know where the families lived and the ages of the kids in the home so I could show them only the products that would be a good fit.

"There's a family with children just a couple doors down," the woman said. Then she added, "But before you go there, I want you to know that her husband died last year."

I learned that the neighbor's husband had been a firefighter in New York City on 9/11. He had run up the stairs of one of the World Trade Center towers before it came crashing down.

"She's a single mom now," the woman explained.

When I knocked on that door, I didn't jump right in with my usual presentation, of course. Because of what I had learned about the situation, when the mom opened the door wearing an NYFD shirt, I said, "Hey, thank you for answering the door. My name is Dave. I've talked to a lot of families this summer, and I'll tell you why I stopped by in just a second. But first I wanted to say thank you for your sacrifice and what your husband did and for all that you've had to deal with over this past year. I think you're awesome." I gave her a high five and then I told her why I was there. I was sincerely grateful for the opportunity to thank her.

Sure enough, she invited me in. I showed her the books and everything we offered to help prepare her children for success. The kids loved the products, and I loved interacting with the kids. Before I left, I gave the mother a hug and then hugged all the kids.

Yes, she bought a bunch of tools to help her children. But I felt fulfilled because I made a difference in their lives. Because I had taken the time to ask questions about the neighbors, I was prepared to serve them well. I did my homework.

That's what makes servant selling different. If you care, you prepare. If you don't, you won't.

Let's Get Connected

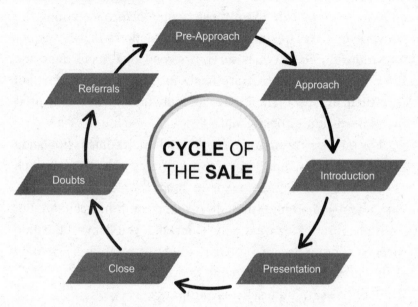

The sales cycle—what we call the Cycle of the Sale at South-western Consulting—starts with the Pre-approach. Everything that happens before the Approach is the Pre-approach. It includes research, lead generation (canvasing buildings, purchasing lists, cold calling), learning about your leads (having conversations), and so on.

The Pre-approach is not flashy. Maybe that's why so many sincere salespeople get it wrong. They think selling is all about demonstrating a product or service or closing with an incredible technique. Those things are important, but they come later in the process. The Pre-approach serves as the foundation for every sales relationship.

The Pre-approach is what sets a servant salesperson apart. Good salespeople will talk to prospects. They'll even be persistent and enthusiastic. But servant salespeople will learn as much as they can about those people *before* beginning the conversation. As a result, the entire interaction will feel warmer and more familiar. When servant salespeople have done the Pre-approach, they are more likely to form a true connection with their prospect. Then they can truly understand their prospect's needs and provide help.

For me, the Pre-approach isn't optional. It comes with being a professional in this line of work. Doing the Pre-approach shows that you actually want to help people. Any time you care about something, you'll do research on it beforehand. For example, if your kids want to take parkour, you'll invest the time to learn about it because you care about your family's activities. Or if you're considering moving to a new neighborhood, you'll probably research the schools and parks.

I didn't do the Pre-approach during my first day on the job, and it was a disaster. It wasn't until I shadowed my sales leader the next day that I understood the importance of learning all I could about my prospects before I approached them. After that, I tried to end every interaction by gathering as much information as possible about the other people in the neighborhood.

My conversations often went something like this:

"Thank you for your time. It would really help if you could tell me a little bit about the families you know in this area. I'm trying to show these educational products to forty-two families today. I don't want to bother families that don't have kids, and I want to make sure to reach the ones that do. So right next door, do they have kids there? No? Okay, cool. I can mark them off. Thank you. You've saved me so much time.

"What about the next house down? Oh, they do have kids? Got it. Little guys or big guys? They've got little ones? Okay.

Like preschool age or elementary? Elementary kids? Cool, I'll talk to them about my products for younger kids and try to help them through what I'm doing. Just so I know, to be polite, who would I ask for over there? The Johnsons? Cool. Parents' names? Do you know them? Just the Johnsons? Okay. That's totally fine.

"What about right next to the Johnsons? Emma Cheng? Got it. Kids? Little guys? Big guys? Oh, you've seen all sorts of older kids over there? So, high school and college age? Thank you. That'll save me a ton of time, and I'll know what to show them. Do you think I can catch them at home during the day? I want to save time and serve them well. Later is better? Thanks."

What did I learn from these interactions?
Whether the families had kids and how old they were.
What to call them when they answered the door.
The best time to knock on the door to reach them.
I learned quickly that the more information I had before I knocked on the door, the better I could serve the family. That's what the Pre-approach is all about.

How Do You Find Leads?

So how do you get started with your Pre-approach? Where can you find names or leads? Some will come from personal referrals and asking your friends and network for referrals. (For more information about the Getting Referrals step in the sales cycle, see chapter 12.) But even without factoring in referrals, you have far more options to generate leads than you think.

Here's a brief list of ideas for lead generation:

Past Counterparts. Call your managers and associates from previous roles or geographical areas to say hi and find out their counterparts in your area of focus or in cities near you.

College Alumni. Many colleges have nationwide directories of where their alumni work. Get in touch with your alumni association and start calling fellow graduates.

Family and Friends. Don't forget these obvious connections. You may be surprised who they know that might be a prospect for you.

Master Client List (Vertical Marketing). List every single client you've had. Go through your list of names line by line and make sure you've searched for each client on Google, LinkedIn, and places like yellowpages.com. Brainstorm whether you might be able to upsell or cross-sell other services to that client. Find other branches/offices to prospect. Look up each person's competition so you can call on them.

National Account List. Create a list of large companies nationwide that need the product or service you are selling. Research connections with and to them.

Pre-loaded Leads. If your company provides you with leads from an automated lead lead-generation tool, be sure to factor these into your Pre-approach strategy.

List of Related Industries. Create a list of related industries. Don't question whether it's a good industry for you to work. Just dial and start asking questions! Begin by calling the biggest companies in each industry and learn something about their business by talking with the gatekeeper.

LinkedIn Search. Use the advanced search techniques to explore your contacts for possible leads. See if your contacts can make an introduction.

Business Journal. Go to the library and ask for the Book of Lists. The librarian will know what it is. This resource will have many companies listed in your area, and some of them might generate leads.

Networking. Nothing beats old-fashioned connecting with people. Organizations like BNI, Chamber of Commerce, Young Professionals, and Meetup.com will enable you to get connected with potential leads. Once you join a group, you'll have access to its upcoming networking events, both in-person and virtual.

SIC Code List. Visit www.infoUSA.com and purchase a list based on the industry SIC code (Standard Industrial Classification) for your target business or consumer market.

Canvassing Buildings. Go to an office park and write down the names of all the companies in the building that might be prospects. Do your Pre-approach homework first and then introduce yourself. You can even reference the names of other people in the same building as you go.

Territory Re-Work. Revisit or call back prospects who blew you off before. Circumstances change. It's especially important to do your homework to discover what may have changed or to reestablish a connection point.

This list is only a starting point, of course. Your circumstances will offer a wider variety of options. When our coaches work with each salesperson, they often develop position-specific lists to generate a wealth of leads.

The More You Know

Once you've identified a potential prospect, however cold or warm they may be, the next step is to get as much information about them as you can. Social media has made this easier than ever. You could see if any of your connections and friends on LinkedIn or Facebook are also connected to your prospect. Then call or email the person you know to get Pre-approach information. If you get a referral to someone, you can ask them for details on the referral.

Another way would be to google the prospect's name and then do a little research. Go to the person's LinkedIn or Facebook page. If you see that they've recently set up a fundraiser for their local Boys and Girls Clubs of America for their birthday on Facebook, that's where you should start the conversation. If you see them at children's birthday parties or in travel photos, you can start there to establish rapport.

Remember, these techniques will help you connect with your prospect and serve them better. Plus, if you can master the Pre-approach, you'll be one of the top people in your company because everybody else wants to skip ahead. So how do you go about improving your Pre-approach skills? Begin by figuring out the most pertinent information you need to know to make a quick connection with your prospects. No matter what business you're in, there are things that would be good to know beforehand to accelerate your connection. Some examples include:

How do you know this person? What do you respect most about them?

Tell me about their family. How many members? How many kids? What are their ages?

Where are they from?

What are they into—yoga, sports, food blogging, grandkids?

What college did they go to?

What's their cell phone number?

What is their income range or socioeconomic status?

When might be the best time to catch them?

Are they quick or slow decision-makers?

Do they tend to ask questions? Are they pretty direct?

There are also industry-specific questions that you will want to add. For example, if you're a Realtor, it would be awesome to know how long your prospect has been in their current house. Knowing these types of things beforehand will save you some time and accelerate the relationship. You might ask:

Why are they moving?

Do they like their current house?

Has the family outgrown the space?

Do they want to move to a different neighborhood?

Do they like the school system?

If you're a mortgage loan officer, your prospect is often that real estate agent. You'll want to know things like:

How much volume do they do?

Do they have others on their team who support them?

Is marketing important to them?

What office do they work for?

What if you're a car salesperson? Here are a few questions that might be vital to get answered in the Pre-approach phase about a prospect:

When was the last time they bought a car?

What do they like about their car?

What do they not like about their car?

What features are most important to them?

Do they need more space in their car?

What's their favorite make and model?

If you're selling insurance, you may want to know:

Who are they currently insured with?

What are they paying for their current insurance?

How many vehicles do they have? How many drivers? Do they own or lease?

Do they own their home?

Do they have life insurance? Long-term care insurance? An umbrella policy?

Or maybe you're a financial advisor looking to bring in a new client. You'll want to find out:

Do they have a current advisor?

What is their job?

When are they planning to retire?

Do they currently have a mortgage?

What plans do they have for the future? (For example, do they want to own a beach house? Travel the world?)

Many home-based businesses depend on building a team of salespeople, so prior to having a recruiting conversation with a prospect you would want to know:

Have they ever been involved in direct sales or a home-based business?

Are they opportunity-minded?

Do they enjoy interacting with people?

Have you heard them share about products they love? If so, what products?

When you do the Pre-approach, at first your focus is more about getting to know the person. After you learn the personal information, you want to find out any specific sales-related information. That's second-level information, though—it's great if you can get sales-related information, but personal information is what you really want at this point.

Servant salespeople care about the people who will be on the other side of the door, on the other end of a call, or sitting on the other side of the table. They care enough to do research on their prospects first so they can connect with them at a deeper level.

Servant salespeople see their prospects as real people—individuals to get to know so they can connect with them in a stronger, more genuine way. Genuine conversation usually leads to authentic connection, which is exactly what servant selling is about: connecting with your prospects as quickly as you can to help them with your product or service.

Putting the Principles into Action

What techniques have you used in the past for the Pre-approach? Which strategies discussed in this chapter can you incorporate into your current plan?

Use the ideas in this chapter as inspiration and write out your own fifteen methods you can use to generate more leads. If you have a coach, discuss your list with them.

No matter what your business is, some things are good to know beforehand to accelerate your connection with your prospects. What is the most pertinent information you need to know to quickly connect with them?

Think about a person who sold you something and provided exceptional service. What types of things did they seem to know about you ahead of time?

CHAPTER 7

APPROACH: COME ALONGSIDE

Bring Your Confidence and Your Care

Have you heard the adages "You never get a second chance to make a first impression" and "You have seven seconds to make a great first impression"? Anyone in sales knows that it's important to make a strong first impression. Otherwise, the deal is done before it begins.

Servant salespeople bring all the great Pre-approach information they collected into their Approach, which is the first interaction with the prospect. This shows the prospect that they are important and valued, and it sets servant salespeople apart from everyone else who has tried to "sell something" to the prospect in the past.

Having a good Pre-approach will calm your nerves during the Approach, enabling you to think more clearly and sound more confident. Bringing the best version of your "sales self" also helps people feel more comfortable with you faster, which ultimately helps and serves them. Then they can make a clearer decision about what you are offering because they're not getting caught up in what ruins most approaches: stammering, stuttering, nervous ticks, lack of eye contact, fast talking, and uncomfortable body language. Coming into the Approach with great "intel" shows your prospects up front that you care about them enough to take the time to prepare.

Servant salespeople recognize that they are not like everyone in the selling profession. They take pride in focusing on others. Their ultimate goal is for the prospect's needs to be met. In the pages ahead, I'll give you strategies and language for effectively approaching your prospects and making connections with them quickly.

What's Your Name Again?

Another vital strategy servant salespeople employ is getting the prospect's name right. Nothing is worse than trying to build rapport with someone when you can't even remember their name. Ask "Jack" about his family when his name is actually Joe, and you'll get an awkward pause in the conversation that screams, "I don't really care about you!" The first time you speak with the client is during the Approach, so it's crucial to show respect by knowing the person's name at this early stage.

If you can't remember someone's name, it's usually because you never knew it in the first place. Here are seven "-tions" for remembering names:

Relaxation. The number one reason we forget a name is because we are stressed out or distracted. Take a deep breath before meeting someone and focus on listening.

Repetition. Repeat someone's name to yourself (silently, in your head) at least five to ten times in the first fifteen seconds to program it into memory. This is especially helpful with unique names that can be hard to forget.

Utilization. Use someone's name three to five times when you're talking to them, especially when you first meet them. For example, "Joe. It's Joe, right? Nice to meet you, Joe. Joe, where are you from?"

Association. Make their first name rhyme with something or create an alliterative pattern. For example, "Hannah banana" or "Angela apple."

Visualization. Mentally overlay a new person's face with the face of someone you know well who has the same name.

Picturization. Remember, pictures are the language of the mind. Many names can be automatically associated with a picture (for example, Reid, Holly, Robin, or Matt).

Finalization. End every conversation by using the person's name. "Very nice meeting you, Mike."

By using these seven "-tions," you'll remember the names of prospects and will never have to be concerned about bumbling names. Then you can focus on making a genuine connection and serving people well.

3-D Names

Servant salespeople always use names in every step of the Cycle of the Sale. They remember names to honor their prospect and build credibility quickly, and they use names to provide testimonials.

The 3-D names technique brings together three things: Name. Fact(s). Story. When using this technique, you reference the name, say a few facts about that name, and then tell a quick story that describes and sells what you do. Here's an example I might use if I was calling to set up a workshop with a new prospect:

Hi Ms. Prospect, let me tell you about Peter McGee [name]. He's the branch manager [fact] at Vision Home Loans [fact] in Tallahassee, Florida [fact]. Like you, he has a far more experienced team than most offices [fact], which is good. But he said that his people have gotten lazy when it comes to actively asking clients for referrals [story that sells what I do].

Peter [name] said they are leaving thousands of dollars on the table every month [story that sells what I do]. So he asked me to present his team with my workshop on referrals—on the importance of asking for them, how to ask consistently, and how to feel good about it. The workshop was such a huge success that Peter's team thanked him [story that sells what I do], and then Peter [name] thanked me for coming [story that sells what I do].

This technique not only builds rapport during the crucial Approach step, but it also connects your new prospect with a past client's solved problems. I might continue the conversation like this:

Also Ms. Prospect, I'd like to tell you about Sara Johnson [name], who leads a very successful team [fact] of insurance agents at Texas Horizon Insurance [fact] in Dallas [fact]. When we first talked, she told me that her people were so reactive rather than proactive during their workdays that few of them followed a plan [fact]. She said the stress most of them feel each day is due to their lack of proper planning [fact].

Sara [name] and I crafted an entire training around time-management tips and techniques that helped her people get more proactive with their schedules [story that sells what I do]. When I completed her workshop, four or five people told me that they couldn't wait to integrate what they had learned. It was exactly what they needed [story that sells what I do].

Then I would tie the 3-D names together—both Peter McGee and Sara Johnson—for my prospect:

So, are you thinking that your team needs help with referrals, like Peter and his group? Or do you think it would be better to cover time-management skills, like we did for Sara and her team? Which would be better for you? Or maybe your team needs help with something I didn't mention, like handling objections and excuses, or mastering closing techniques. What area do you think would be best for them to have some extra reinforcement?

Note how I gave Ms. Prospect another Question Cluster. Remember, at this step in the sales cycle, I'm just trying to get the person talking. Later, when I'm wrapping up the 3-D story, I'll say something like this:

Yeah, Peter had his whole team sign up, and they've had their biggest year ever. Sara had four of her agents sign up. What's really cool is that one of those agents on her team, Myra Alvarez, has been in the office for just two years—and Myra is already beating everyone who's been there for twenty years. Sara told me a couple times this coaching thing works!

Name. Fact. Story. The reason I call it a 3-D name is that this technique makes the name pop off the page or out of the phone and brings it to life. It's much more than name-dropping. I call it third-party selling because that 3-D name is doing the selling for me!

I've often explained it to new salespeople this way: Think of all these 3-D names as a team of servant sellers lined up behind you in conversations with prospects, ready to sell for you. Everyone you've served in the past becomes a 3-D name. When you seek to serve your prospect and you use names three-dimensionally, good things are likely to take place.

By using 3-D names effectively throughout the sale, you can silence a lot of concerns before they start. After all, when you use this technique it's not you talking—it's your army of people building your credibility and making the sale for you. *Don't listen to me. Listen to him. Listen to her.*

Know What to Say

The Approach step in the Cycle of the Sale comes down to two things: what you say and what you don't say. You need to know what you're going to say when you approach your prospect. And to do that, you must get scripted. Some people use the words *sales talks*, *talk tracks*, or *talking points* to describe scripts. Either way, these preplanned and strategic words will help you know what to say next.

It may seem counterintuitive, but by investing the time to memorize a sales track or script, you are serving your prospects well. Having confidence in a memorized, proven talk script allows you to focus on *listening* to what your prospect is actually saying rather than *worrying* about what you are going to say next.

Another great reason to be scripted is, ironically, so that you don't say too much. I've found that during the Approach, the right mix of conversation is 25 percent talking and 75 percent listening.

(That's at a minimum—try listening even more than that.) Scripts not only tell you what you should say when you speak, but they also give you the freedom to shut up and listen. One of the greatest mistakes salespeople make at this stage is talking too much. That's why it's so important to keep the 25/75 ratio in mind.

Not everyone adapts to using scripts. After being part of a business that has coached more than twenty thousand individuals, I have found that the people who use scripts almost always experience greater success. The people who try to do it their own way usually struggle.

Some salespeople have gotten away from using scripts because they don't want to sound like they are speaking in a canned way. But scripting is just programming. It's using words that you know work. Being scripted doesn't mean you're not genuine; it simply means you're prepared because you care about connecting. Once you have the scripting down, *then* you can free yourself to customize it for your prospect—focusing on their needs first with the servant mindset—while putting your own brilliance and personality into it.

Let me demonstrate with a script I use all the time when calling a new prospect from a referral:

> Is this Nick? Hey, Nick. This is Dave, Dave Brown. If you're trying to put a face and a name together real quick, it's probably not going to work because we actually haven't met yet. Cool. Yeah. I heard some good things about you from Julia Robinson, actually. Julia said a lot of awesome stuff [then I list the details I learned in the Pre-approach. Does that name help me or hurt me?

I've used this script so many times that it's become second nature to me. By following the script, I don't have to think about my next words. I can focus on the conversation and interaction instead, which honors my prospect. And because I know the script so well, I've been able to add a few personal tweaks to make it my own. For example, the "help me or hurt me" reference is my addition. Typically, the person will say, "Oh, yeah, so-and-so is great. It helps you." The question is more rhetorical; I've never had anyone respond negatively. It simply allows me to get a read on their relationship with the source of the referral, and it gets them talking, nodding along with me, affirming the relationship and, by implication, me.

Another addition I've made to my script is to say, "I heard some good things about you," because I love to build people up. I don't say this if I haven't talked to anyone about the person, as that would be disingenuous. I do this strictly when I am working referrals, which is most of the time.

The only way to get better at the talking part of the Approach is to practice. Study your scripts/talk tracks, reading them over and over. You may need to get creative to make them part of your life. For example, I used to study scripts as I worked out. I would do my push-ups, then study our phone-approach script. I would do a series of sit-ups on my foam roller, then study another call script. I would do my pull-ups and study scripts for handling objections over the phone. Then I would start over and review the scripts again.

Another valuable way to practice your Approach is to engage in role-playing. Once you're familiar with the scripts, you can go back and forth with somebody on your team. Or practice with your family or kids. Whatever works.

Learn to Get Them Talking

The old adage is true: God gave us two ears and one mouth for a reason—to listen twice as much as we talk. Keep this in mind as you use your servant selling approach. Allow your client to do the talking; everyone loves to talk, especially about themselves. Plus, it's hard for people to hang up or walk away from somebody who is asking them questions. People feel more comfortable with others who are *genuinely* trying to connect with them. It makes them feel important.

The second piece of the Approach step is to learn what *not* to say. As I mentioned, during 75 percent of the conversation, you should be listening while your prospect is talking. But how do you ensure they do most of the talking? It's not as difficult as you might think, but that's only *if* you go about it the right way—by asking questions.

Remember, if you've already done your Pre-approach, you know at least a little bit about the person. The quicker you can start asking questions to get them talking, the better. That's another reason I added the question in the previous script, "Does that name help me or hurt me?" I'll usually follow up by asking, "How do you know Julia? How long have you known her? Do you guys work together or are you just friends?" My aim is to encourage the prospect to talk, not just about anything, but about himself.

So many inexperienced salespeople make the mistake of rushing to the Demonstration step and bypassing the Pre-approach and the Approach steps. But in my experience, the majority of the sale gets done in these initial steps if you slow down and get to know your customer. Patiently going through the Pre-Approach and Approach allows you to know your customer's needs, so you can better serve them in the Demonstration step.

One of the most effective ways to ask questions is to use the Question Cluster. Virgie Sandford, a successful district sales manager for Southwestern Advantage, uses this powerful sales technique.

A Question Cluster puts several questions together. I used this technique in my follow-up example earlier: "How do you know Julia? How long have you known her? Do you guys work together or are you just friends?" I asked this as a bundle of questions intentionally. But why?

A quick question leads to a quick answer, but a clustered question leads to a longer, fuller answer. Here's why. When someone asks you one question, you focus on that single question. You don't start thinking about related topics because your brain hasn't been asked to do that. But when you encounter a cluster of questions, it's not that simple. Your brain begins to seek connections and context to answer them all. As a result, this technique powerfully primes the prospect's "talking pump" and drops sales gold all over the place.

A simple example is asking about someone's family. You might say, "So tell me about your family. How many kids do you have? Tell me about each one. What are they into? How old are they? What do they like to do? Just tell me about the family."

Ideally, you want to cluster four to seven quick, related questions. Start with a general question or comment, insert some detailed questions, and then finish by returning to the general question or comment.

After being asked a Question Cluster, people often reply, "Whew. Yeah." And then they relax and sigh, as if to say, "Wow! I get to talk." This almost always happens when you use the Question Cluster the right way.

Usually, when people start talking to me and sharing their answers to the Question Cluster, I haven't even gotten to my reason for calling. That's exactly what you want at this stage. You're just genuinely engaging about a connection you share or something that's important to your prospect, which helps them feel more comfortable with you. You're learning their cadence of conversation so that you can fit right in with them. You're honoring them and adapting to them, which is another important aspect of servant selling.

What should you do while they are talking? You should be taking notes. Literally. Certainly, it's important to take mental notes too, but I encourage salespeople to take written or typed notes as they listen. I talk this through with my prospects, saying, "I don't want to miss anything, so I'm going to take notes." Sometimes I'll even bring it up later in the conversation, saying that if they hear me typing over the phone it's because I don't want to miss anything.

Ask. Listen. And write it down.

When you're truly listening to someone, you are showing them respect, which is the highest form of service. Most people are distracted by what's going on in their lives, so they don't pay enough attention to the person they are talking to. Servant salespeople understand the importance of giving their full attention to their prospects, showing they care more about their prospects than themselves.

Slow Down to Speed Up

I had this lesson reinforced to me several years ago when I was meeting with my mentor, Henry Bedford, the chairman and CEO of Southwestern Family of Companies. We had just finished breakfast together and were on our way to a meeting together. It was right around the time that all the Southwestern Advantage young adults return to our headquarters after a summer of selling, so there were many college students in the building. As we headed up the stairs, we encountered one of the young men in the stairwell.

The student was nineteen years old and ready to start his sophomore year in college. When he saw us, he stuck out his hand and greeted Henry: "Hi, Mr. Bedford. You spoke at Sales School." He gave his name, and Henry replied, "Oh, nice to meet you." I thought that was going to be it because we were running late to get upstairs for our meeting. But the young guy kept talking.

"Yeah, I think this program is really cool. I'm looking forward to next summer."

"How did you do out there?" Henry asked.

The student told us he had sold 1,200 units. If you remember from earlier, the top performers sold at least 12,000, and I had sold more than 18,000 in one summer. He was clearly not a superstar salesperson.

I decided to introduce myself in hopes we could wrap up the meet and greet. "My name is Dave Brown."

He knew my name and said it was an honor to meet me too.

"Yeah, man, nice to meet you," I said. "We're running up to a meeting."

I'm sure my body language conveyed that we should move on. Then Henry did something completely unexpected. He started asking the student questions: "Tell me about your summer. Who was your leader? How did it go? What did you learn?"

I immediately recognized his use of the Question Cluster. Clearly, Henry wanted to get a thoughtful response, not simply a yes or no.

Sure enough, the guy started talking. He went on and on about his experience, offered feedback on his sales manager, described the interesting people he met, and gave all sorts of other information. Then he said, "Oh, and I actually had some ideas for the product."

I confess by then I was thinking, *You haven't sold much product. How would you have good ideas for it?*

Henry calmly replied, "Oh, that's great. We love ideas for improvement. We're always trying to get better here." Apparently, the young guy had some digital marketing experience and felt he could offer his insight.

As Henry patiently listened and nodded, I didn't hear much of what was being said. To be candid, I was annoyed. Henry acted like the ideas were good, but I walked away and responded to the calls and texts reminding me I had only a limited window of time with my CEO.

Finally, after thirty minutes in the stairwell, Henry concluded the conversation, and we headed up the stairs. He could tell I was frustrated with the delay and stopped me.

"Whoa, whoa, whoa," he said. "What did I just do for that kid?"

"You listened to him," I replied. "I get it. I get what you were doing."

Henry shook his head. "No, what did I just do for that kid?"

I stopped to think. "Well, you made him feel important."

Henry started nodding with me as I began putting the pieces together.

"He probably felt like there were no barriers for him here," I admitted. "And that his ideas are valued at the top. You're the CEO of this company and were very easy to talk to. You were asking him questions and getting to know him. You showed him that he was more important than anything you had going on, and you put his feelings and desires before your own."

"Yes," Henry responded as we headed toward the meeting again. "And that's my ultimate job here—to make everyone feel important and know that their voice matters."

That conversation in the stairwell impressed upon me the importance of genuinely engaging every single person in an authentic way. Henry was serving that young man by learning more about him and his story. As a result, that guy was far more likely to continue the sales program the following year and refer others to do the same.

What stops salespeople from investing the time and energy to engage? The number one reason salespeople do not have these types of unhurried conversations is simple: they're lazy. They know they should, but they don't feel like it.

A second reason is that they think it's a waste of time. They think if they can just tune their presentation skills or be ready to deal with doubts, they don't need to properly listen and engage. That may work some of the time, but they'll never experience breakthrough success if they don't honor their prospects by listening.

To be fair, some salespeople might not understand the importance of engaging with their prospects. Maybe they've never been taught why servant selling is so critical and how to go about it. For others, it might be a time-management issue. They genuinely think they don't have time to connect. But when they do connect, they'll move quickly through the sales cycle, and everything will become so much easier.

Go Low and Slow

I'm a high-energy kind of guy, but most people aren't like me. I'd say just 25 percent of the customers I've sold to in person match my pace. I love it when I interact with those people. We have some fun, tell stories, and joke around. But the majority of people I interact with are naturally more deliberate, reserved, or measured than I am. And that's okay.

When I first started selling, it took me a few weeks to realize I needed to change my approach. With the servant selling mindset, it's not about me—it's about my prospect. I was going a million miles an hour, sprinting from porch to porch and talking fast. But I wasn't connecting with people. I didn't know their needs. After I had gone through my presentation, they would ask, "So, what are you doing here again?" Sigh.

They weren't listening because I wasn't listening. They were looking at my shoes or shirt—basically doing anything but paying attention! And to be honest, I wasn't learning about them because I was going so fast.

I finally embraced this critical lesson: During the Approach step, go low and slow. Intentionally use a lower, softer tone of voice that feels unthreatening. It subtly lets your prospects feel like they are in charge of the conversation, and it honors them by letting them dictate the pace.

How slow? Well, for me it was a dramatic change. I had to slow my pace by what felt like 100 percent. It felt uncomfortable for me to talk so slowly, but I realized that people need time to process the information.

I like to tell people that when you find a pace that feels awkward and uncomfortable for you, then you *might* be getting close to the right pace. Remember this: you've practiced your Approach so many times that you are probably talking way too fast (especially if you are nervous). Listening isn't high on your prospect's priority list either. If you're in person, they're looking at what you're wearing. If you're on the phone, they probably just stepped away from doing something else, like checking email, and are wondering who you are and what you want. You've just inserted yourself into their life, so you need to give them time to take it all in.

I probably would have missed out on most of my sales if I hadn't shifted to talking low and slow during my Approach. Once I stopped focusing on myself and started thinking about what made my prospect comfortable, everything changed.

When I train larger groups of salespeople, I spend most of my time the first day of training just getting people to slow down. This honors the prospect. By choosing to go low and slow in the Approach step, you also project confidence. Every conversation is a dance. You lead by asking a question or deploying a Question Cluster. You know when they're done with their sentence because you're listening for where the periods are in the conversation. You don't step on their toes by talking over them. The last thing you want to do is talk over one another and end up having an awkward exchange: "Oh, okay. Oh, no. No, you go first." Any time someone has to say, "You first," the conversation is off to a horrible start. By going low and slow, you stay out of the way and let the person dictate the pace. Then you adapt to what works for them.

By engaging in the conversation at their pace and their cadence, you serve them.

The Wow/How Technique

When you meet prospects for the first time, you need to be able to offer a brief description of what you do. You want it to be punchy but clear, inspiring but not cheesy. Most importantly, you want to be able to share it with conviction. You must be able to communicate your genuine passion for what you offer and why you feel that it helps people. People will catch your passion for making a difference if you're genuine in how you share it.

The Wow/How Technique helps you create this scripted answer that explains what you offer to others when someone asks, "What do you do?" Your answer should make them say, "*Wow*, that's cool. *How* do you do that?" Remember, the more clearly you present yourself, the more you serve your prospects. Making it easy for them to understand and catch the vision is not only good for your business, it's also helpful to them.

For example, financial planners might say, "I help people become financially literate." The prospect could reply, "Wow, that's great. How do you do that?" Then the planner could say something like, "Do you remember opening your first 401(k) and how overwhelming all the terms and options were with investing? [Pause for an answer.] I help people learn about their investment options and help them plan for their future retirement and other endeavors. Do you feel prepared for your retirement? [Listen and take mental notes.] Do you have a business card? Let's connect sometime soon for a cup of coffee."

Here's another example of an encounter that happened to me recently. I met a caterer named Alex at an event in Nashville. Alex was starting his own business. When I asked about his work, he answered, "I make party hosts look like culinary geniuses."

"Cool, how do you do that?" I asked.

Alex replied, "When I prepare food for any event, I take time on the front end to get to know the host and their personality and what vibe they want. Then I customize the eating experience for the guests based on what I find out. I don't specialize in one style of food—I adjust my style around what my clients want."

He asked me if I ever host larger events, and I said, "Yes!"

"When's your next event?" he asked.

I gave him my business card and told him to follow up with me. "Well done!" I told him. Indeed, he was our caterer the next time we had our entire team in town.

The Wow/How Technique can work for any industry, so apply it to your own setting and script it out. Run it by your manager or peers to get feedback, then put it to work for you.

Get Your Stories Straight

One critical tool that every servant salesperson needs is the ability to tell stories, especially during the Approach. The best salespeople in the world are the best storytellers. Storytelling is one of the oldest ways humans communicate with each other. Becoming a better storyteller will help you connect more easily with those around you. It will enhance your relationships and propel your business to new levels of engagement and success. In fact, everyone who's sold anything of substance probably used stories to do it.

Religious leaders throughout history have used stories to convey truths and move people to action. Politicians use stories to sell their campaign messaging. Cultural leaders incorporate stories in their speeches. Even social media makes it easy to post "stories." We are wired to want stories. If you're not using stories to sell, you're not serving people well because you're ignoring a fundamental human need. The salesperson's job is to bring the future to life for the prospect, and it's hard to do that without telling stories to color that future.

Stories add an emotional charge to your conversations. At Southwestern, we're famous for saying, "Selling is a transference of emotion." If you want to tap into emotions when you're selling, you must master the art of storytelling—especially when you're trying to engage someone during the Approach. Nothing pulls the heartstrings like a good story.

Everyone has funny or interesting things that have happened in their life or career they can draw upon. To be a great storyteller, you need a repertoire of stories you can recall from memory. This way, no matter what the situation or social event, you'll be an engaging communicator and can easily connect with the people around you.

Think of an interesting story from your childhood or your first job. What are all the possible lessons you can learn from the story? With a little preparation, you can use the same story in several different scenarios. A few years ago, I attended a conference for the National Speakers Association (NSA), and they encouraged speakers to collect a repertoire of 100 stories. If you can draw five different lessons from each of those stories, you'll have a story prepared for 500 separate occasions. This number can include slight variations on the original story. Keep track of your stories by writing them in the notes section of your phone or on a notepad so that storytelling becomes a natural part of your sales process. If you embrace this technique throughout the sales cycle, you won't just be talking about your-self or rambling for no reason. You'll have a well-structured anecdote that engages your prospects with focus and purpose.

Using stories in this way will take practice, which is why so few salespeople do it well. But servant selling isn't about what makes you comfortable. It's about how to best serve your prospect.

Think carefully about each of the stories in your repertoire. Remember these three important steps to crafting a great story:

- Keep the lesson or point in mind to make it as concise as possible.
- Identify the essential components. Nonessential elements only clutter the story and distract from the point you really want to make.
- Use your facial expressions and tone of voice to breathe life into the story and reenact it.

One thing I love to do as I take the Approach step is to review my prospect list or business development list. I try to identify at least two stories to tell each prospect on my list. I think about what I know of their situation and comb through my memory bank for similar people I've sold to in the past. Who has a similar background? Who overcame similar challenges in the past? Where can I insert some emotion into the conversation by sharing a story that fits their life situation?

My aim is not merely to tell a story. I'm not there to entertain people. My aim is to tell a story with purpose—one that builds rapport, establishes credibility, connects the prospect with other people who have purchased previously, or affirms the need and shows empathy. Get intentional about telling stories well and using them at the right time and in the right way, and you will have excellent sales results.

Putting the Principles into Action

Create your own Wow/How description to use during the Approach. Write it out. Try it on your peers, manager, or coach to get feedback. Refine and practice it until it becomes natural. The key is to know it so well that you can use it to engage with and listen to your prospect. When you're not worried about what you're going to say, you will serve them better.

What are some questions you want to ask your prospect in this Approach step? How can you cluster those questions to encourage them to open up and share more about themselves? Create five Question Clusters you can use on a regular basis.

Develop your own story bank that will serve you in several different situations and for different purposes. Have personal stories ready to go as well as stories of previous customers who have experienced success in a variety of key sales categories.

CHAPTER 8

INTRODUCTION: BUILD RAPPORT AND IDENTIFY NEEDS

Have a Heart Intent on Helping

A few years ago, I was referred to Brad Baynum by his son, Taylor. Brad owns and operates a successful line of restaurants called Pizza King in the southern part of Delaware. Brad has many team members, a number of managers, and a handful of general managers who lead each location.

Once I got Brad on the phone, we connected around personal development and the importance of working on ourselves as leaders. He admitted to me that he hadn't done enough leadership training with his top team members but didn't know if signing them up for leadership coaching was the right move. Eight months into a worldwide pandemic at the time, he, like almost every restaurant owner, was just getting by. He said throughout our conversations that he didn't know if we had a fit, but I stuck with him.

I kept asking him specific questions about each of his general managers, including what their strengths and weaknesses were. I also asked him about his next level of management and who he had "on the bench" in case one of his key leaders left. Then we started talking about what he struggled with in terms of guiding his leaders and motivating the next generation of team members (millennials and Gen Zers) he was hiring daily.

As we spoke more, we got closer personally and professionally, and he started to trust me. This is what naturally happens when you are discovering your prospect's needs with a heart intent on helping.

Brad was interested in getting help, but he needed more time and answers to get there. Over the course of four or five calls, I learned quite a bit about his business and his family. He opened up about the need for his managers to evolve into leaders who would hold themselves and their employees accountable. He also told me that it was a challenge to retain reliable team members. As we continued to speak, Brad started to understand that the problems we uncovered could be improved by getting himself and his GMs into coaching with us.

I told him stories of other leaders we had worked with, and he began to get more and more excited about seeing those results for himself. I presented a leadership workshop for him and his GMs, and it was a success. Both Brad and Laura, another great leader of his company, signed up for coaching, and they have been growing and coming up with creative ways to lead their business forward in volatile times.

After our workshop, Brad said to me, "Thank you for caring enough about me and my business to set up this workshop and help get me and Laura into coaching. The first couple of calls we had together, I was a 1 on a scale of 1–10 for doing this because of all that we had going on and how the world was. But you stuck with me and kept asking me so many dang questions that I eventually sold myself on it."

Questions are your answer. Never forget it.

Questions Are Your Answer

Throughout the first two steps in the Cycle of the Sale—the Pre-Approach and the Approach—you've heard about the importance of asking questions. But in this third step, the Introduction, it's time to strategically increase your questions.

The Introduction starts when you have made the initial connection with your prospect, and they have agreed to proceed with the sales conversation. It's the first real engagement you have with the person about your product or service, and it's your introduction to what their needs may be. In the Introduction step, you focus on questioning, qualifying, and probing. You could call it the "fact-finding" part of the sale. If the Pre-approach is the research step and the Approach is the initial impression, then the Introduction is where you find out the prospect's needs through a series of questions and lots of careful listening.

This is the step of the sales cycle where you build rapport. Sometimes rapport and finding needs go hand in hand, and sometimes they are separate, depending on your product and service. Depending on the length of your sales cycle, you may talk for twenty minutes, you may make four or five calls like I did with Brad, or you may spend twenty months building rapport to even give you a chance at earning your prospect's business.

Once the rapport is built during the Introduction, you move on to finding your prospect's need. Servant salespeople honor their prospects by intentionally slowing down the process to focus on the Introduction. I learned early on to resist the urge to bypass the Introduction and rush to the next step, the Demonstration. Every sale I've ever made has been the result of putting my focus on the Introduction. You certainly need to demonstrate and then close; otherwise, nothing gets sold. But I always say that the Introduction is where the sale gets made.

As you question, qualify, and probe, you will learn what you need to tactically sell your prospects. Often people don't know they have a need, so you can bring it to life for them through your strategic questioning—just like I did with Brad.

Servant salespeople don't go to the next step of the sales cycle unless they find their prospects have a need for their product or service. Sometimes their prospects don't even know they have a need, and often, servant salespeople discover the need during the Introduction because they have helped others with similar challenges.

Back in the day, I often knocked on doors and discovered that the people who answered weren't parents with kids living in the home—they were grandparents. "Oh, educational products," they would say. "I have my kids and grandkids over fairly often."

I would help the grandparents find their need by asking, "Do you get them presents for birthdays and Christmas?"

"Well, sure I do!" they would say.

I would follow up with a question: "Have you ever thought about giving them educational tools, something to help them long after they're tired of playing with a new toy?"

Usually the person would reply, "Oh, we've given some of that stuff before."

Then I asked, "Do they like computer games?"

"They're always on the computer when I'm over there."

"Awesome!" I would say, preparing to talk about our digital options. "Have you ever thought about . . ."

You get the idea. There's no way I could have made all those sales if I didn't engage grandparents in this way. I also sold to aunts, uncles, and even families who didn't have any kids but wanted to bless their friends who had kids. It was all still driven by asking questions because, when it comes to selling, questions are your answer.

Too many salespeople rush through the Introduction step. They get nervous about what the prospect might want and forget that they have a duty to serve by bringing their prospect's needs to light.

If you want to serve other people well, you must uncover a need, strategically ask questions, and then deliver the solution.

Create a Buying Atmosphere

The first thing you must do in the Introduction is create a buying atmosphere where the prospect has the freedom to say no. As we discussed in chapter 1, a lot of people see salespeople as pushy, and that isn't what servant selling is about. The Introduction step should always include this counterintuitive technique.

Why is it counterintuitive? Some people think that the last thing they would want to do is give a prospect the opportunity to say no. But instead of being afraid of receiving a no, servant salespeople should highlight the possibility at the outset. This creates a buying atmosphere. If a prospect feels threatened or pushed into a decision, chances are good that they'll resist. Wouldn't you?

Here's how you create a buying atmosphere that increases the likelihood your prospect will say yes. It's based on the simple truth that people are more likely to say yes if they know it's okay to say no. Put another way, when you give them the freedom to say no, they're more likely to say yes.

When I'm on a sales call, after I've built rapport with the person and started to find the need, I might say something like this: "Jerome, I'm going to tell you about a really cool workshop that Madison [our shared connection] conducted. It might be a fit for you. If it is, we'll get you set up and rock the house. If it's not, no problem. We don't have to do it. Whatever you decide is totally fine."

That's it. This simple technique allows the person to relax and gives them a sense of control over the situation. It does feel counterintuitive, for sure. But if you really care about the person you are trying to help, then you won't want to pressure them into buying something that isn't the right fit.

I even use this technique again later in the sale to reinforce the right buying atmosphere. For example, I might say, "Whatever you decide is totally fine, Jerome. I want you to get into coaching because I know it changes people's lives. But if you choose not to, you won't hurt my feelings. I had my emotions surgically removed last month." The joke keeps it light, and the technique keeps the focus on them. It's not about me. The more they know that the better. As a servant salesperson, you want to communicate that you are there to help and that you're unaffected by the outcome. Creating a buying atmosphere with everyone you sell to reminds your prospects (and you) that they are more important than the sale.

There is something subtle yet powerful in acknowledging that it's okay to say no. Maybe people are moved to act when they feel like the option could be taken away, giving them a little fear of missing out (FOMO). Maybe it's letting them know at the beginning of the buying process that they are in control. Whatever the reason, it moves them to make a decision, especially if you frame it that way explicitly. It also honors the person by allowing them to state their needs.

When selling educational systems, I couldn't afford to get a maybe. I needed to get the opportunity in front of as many people as possible each day. Going back to a house a second time was out of the question. So I often framed it this way:

> If it's for you, awesome. We'll get you signed up like these other families I've had the honor of serving and talking to. If it's not for you, that's totally fine. You're not going to hurt my feelings.
>
> If I can ask for your help with one thing, it would be to just give me a big yes or a big no at the end. Please don't give me a maybe because maybes keep us all stuck. I have to show these systems to thirty families today. So I'm just going to keep moving. Nos are fine. I told you I love nos. They're great. If this [product/service] is for you, awesome. If not, totally cool. Is it okay to request no maybes?

It may or may not be a good fit to frame the decision in this way, depending on your industry. Check with your manager or peers for input. But however you frame it, when you create the best buying atmosphere as you begin the Introduction, you'll be far more likely to hear *yes*.

CLASP

In Southwestern Consulting's business and coaching program, we use an important acronym to guide our questioning during the Introduction: CLASP. This technique will help you to better care for your prospect by asking a targeted series of questions. Following CLASP also streamlines the sales process and provides you with the momentum you need to move to the next steps in the sales cycle. Remember, servant salespeople want to gather as much information as they can about their prospect so they don't push the wrong products or miss a chance to serve.

C: Current. This first step begins with asking what your prospect is *currently* doing. You want to find out where they are at present. I suggest using the Question Cluster technique here again. If I'm talking one-on-one with somebody about coaching, I might say, "Tell me about you. What's your current personal development strategy? Are you currently in a coaching program? Do you attend seminars? Do you like to read personal development books? Currently, what do you do?" Then they tell me.

L: Like. Next, find out what they *like* about what they're doing. You want to give them freedom to say good things about their situation. If they're in another coaching program, for example, ask what is going well.

In the Introduction step, you're learning about what they like and what their hot buttons or selling points are. You're also connecting with them in a way that few people have before. Oftentimes, salespeople go right to saying, "Let me show you how much better we are." But by letting them talk about what works for them, you're connecting so you can better serve your prospects. When this happens, they start to open up.

Some salespeople will be afraid to ask questions about their prospect's current situation and what the prospect likes about it because they are concerned their product or service won't measure up. Don't worry about that. Just ask the question. This part of servant selling is about connecting.

A: Alter. Once your prospect has told you about their current situation and what they like about it, it's time to transition to the need. What would they *alter* or change? These questions get the prospect thinking about the problems they're experiencing with their current situation. This helps the person verbalize reasons for making a change.

S: Signer. The next step would be to find out who has the decision-making power. You want to identify the *signer* early in the process. You should know if the person you are dealing with has the authority to make the purchase or sign the agreement, or if there is anyone else who needs to be included in the conversation.

Most salespeople ask the direct question: "Are you the decision-maker here?" But that approach puts people on the defensive and usually makes them uncomfortable. That's not service. *Whoa*, they might think, *what are you implying?*

Instead, I suggest utilizing the final step in the CLASP acronym:

P: Paint Their Picture. This means review all the stuff you just learned and go back to the start to paint a vivid *picture* for them. We usually say something like this:

> If I'm reading you right, Amir, you're telling me that you're currently comfortable with your volume of sales, you live a great life, and most of the time you are happy with your work.
>
> And what you said you like about your business right now is that you are getting good referrals from your clients. You're staying busy and not getting caught up in a scarcity mentality like most people in your industry. Is that correct?
>
> One thing you said you would alter was facing your fears of recruiting more people so you could grow the

right way. You told me it makes you feel anxious about whether they would be loyal, and you worry about adequately transferring your knowledge to others and hoping they stick around. Did I catch all that?

Perfect. If I can keep all the things that you like the same, building off the amazing referral systems you have created by helping you build similar working systems in every other part of your business . . .

And if I can teach you some recruiting techniques for finding the right people and setting proper expectations in the interview process that will increase their loyalty and buy-in alongside how to delegate properly . . .

If I can do all those things, could you make a decision today? Or is there somebody else who needs to be involved in this conversation before we get you going with coaching?

Notice how I painted the picture of what life would be like with my service or product and then transitioned to the signer question. The focus is not on the prospect's authority but on what the future can look like for them. It would also be helpful to know if they need to check with anybody else before moving forward.

At this point, you're going to get one of two answers. You might hear, "Yeah, you can do all those things with me." If so, great. You would know what to do next, right? Just continue with the sales cycle.

On the other hand, if Amir says, "I'd have to get my partners together," then you can set up the next meeting time. "Great," you could say. "What do we need to do to get them together?" By asking the signer question during the Introduction step, you've saved yourself—and your prospect—a lot of time and energy because you're not trying to close someone who can't even make the decision.

Stay on Track

A word of caution: as you ask questions, make sure your conversations don't take detours that are irrelevant to the process. You're not looking to chat about anything and everything during the Introduction step. For example, if you discover that the prospect went to the same university as your mother, resist the temptation to follow up with, "What dorm did you live in?" That's not relevant. Learning where your prospect went to college does enable you to make a personal connection, though. You can simply mention your mother and perhaps plant a testimonial from someone you've worked with who also attended that university.

Stay focused on the goal of serving by selling. If the conversation goes off course, redirect it with respect. Use phrases like, "In service to you, Sophia, let's talk about . . ." Or, "I could talk all day with you about [the off-track topic], but in service to you, let's focus on . . ." You are a steward of the conversation, and you want to manage it well. If you've done a good job with your Pre-approach and Approach, you will have plenty of information to ask questions that pull your prospect back to the CLASP method.

Remember, the Introduction step is where most of the sale is made. Although you may initially feel like you're spending too much time in the Introduction, it allows you to accelerate the sale in the long run, which will save you and your prospect time. As you're engaging them in questions and conversation, you're telling them a little about your product or service too.

That's what CLASP is designed to do—position you to briefly demonstrate what you're selling so you can later move to the

Closing step with someone who feels comfortable with you. By following these steps, you will show your prospect that you'll only sell them on something they really need.

Don't Skip the Introduction

I won't belabor this point, but it deserves to be highlighted here because it happens all the time. Often, an inexperienced salesperson will skip the Introduction because someone pressures them to move things along. "Just give me the bottom line," the prospect might say. "I don't have much time, so what are you selling?" When the salesperson hurriedly moves to the Demonstration step, they get a quick answer: "Not interested. Seen that. Done that."

The salesperson thinks they're serving the prospect by doing what the prospect says they want. But people often don't realize you're providing something they need. That's why you must show them in this Introduction step. Without the context of a relationship, the prospect will compare your brief presentation of the product or service with their own faulty understanding of their need and other perceived solutions.

If someone insists you get to the point and tell them what you're selling, respond by gently using the CLASP technique. You can say something like, "I totally get that. What do you guys currently have in place around this?"

The truth is that if someone is totally unwilling to go through the process with you, then they just might be a no. That's not a big deal. It takes you one step closer to your No Goal. But most people you meet won't be completely closed to the idea. Most people you'll meet will benefit from going through the Introduction, where you will uncover their need. If you were a doctor assessing someone's health, and he or she told you to just skip the examination (Introduction) and jump to the diagnosis

(Demonstration), you wouldn't do it. So why do the same thing when you're selling? Until you know more about your prospect's situation and needs, you can't present your solution in a way that makes sense.

Years ago, Southwestern Consulting recruited a young, spunky, and personable woman named Gena Parker. She was a talented salesperson, but she often forged ahead during the sales cycle, skipping the Introduction. She'd say, "This is what I'm about. This is what I'm doing. You need to do it because it will help you." It was hard to watch her try to sell for a while. The technique didn't go over well. After Emmie and I worked with her for hours on the servant selling principles, however, she started to understand.

Now Gena has mastered the Cycle of the Sale and routinely achieves great results. She learned that if you really want to serve someone, you'll slow down and follow the process. One evening, she said to me, "I think I'm getting it. Sales is not about having all the answers—it's about asking the right questions. When they're talking, I'm selling." I couldn't have said it better. Gena has gone on to be one of the best in the world at slowing down, listening, and letting her prospects sell themselves as they are talking.

That's true service.

Putting the Principles into Action

Create a list of questions to ask about your prospect's current situation. Don't be afraid to ask. Just be prepared so you know how to respond when you transition to what they would alter if they could.

Remember to connect with intent. During the Introduction, you're doing more than just finding out if there is a need—you are connecting with your prospect so you can serve them better.

Practice painting the picture for your prospect. Imagine people in different life and business scenarios and paint the picture. Practice it until you can easily cast a vision that brings success to life. Then try it in your real-world prospecting.

Craft your own buying atmosphere by creating a script around what you have learned in this chapter. Use this script when you are speaking to your prospects.

CHAPTER 9

DEMONSTRATION: SHARE YOUR SOLUTION

People Love to Buy but Hate to Feel Sold

A couple of years ago, Emmie and I were in Cancún, Mexico, at a place that I'm going to call "Starlight Palace." We were recruited to listen to a demonstration by the resort representatives for a "shared ownership" opportunity with their property. Maybe you have sat through one of these presentations and can envision our situation.

The staff offered us some great perks if we would give them a chance to sell us on their property. The salespeople got to know a little—very little—about us personally over a delicious meal, and then we went to see the property. We were whisked around from villa to villa, seeing everything they had to offer. During the process, there wasn't much connection with us or our own real estate ownership strategy.

Emmie and I have talked many times about what's important to us regarding real estate. We would have been happy to speak freely about it with any one of the people we met that day—if they would have taken the time to ask and learn about what we wanted. Instead, we were shown *this* perk and *that* feature mixed with this *other* amazing thing. It was a dog and pony show, with almost zero interest shown in us, the potential "shared owners." They emphasized how popular we would be with our friends, who would join us at this beachfront paradise.

We were directed to take a seat at the "get-down-to-business" desk. The salespeople asked if we liked the property, and we said, "Yes, it's a very nice place." Then over the next forty-five minutes, they asked us to buy all sorts of different options, demonstrated by multiple people. Every time they asked us to buy this or that, we answered, "Sorry, we don't want to buy into shared ownership." We must have said, "We don't want to do this" ten times because we were not interested. Like I said before, they would have known that if they had asked.

We walked away from "an opportunity of a lifetime" that day, knowing that our hosts were disappointed by our lack of interest in buying—and knowing that they didn't care about us as people one bit. They had skipped the crucial Introduction step and gone straight to the Demonstration.

I wasn't surprised. A lot of salespeople avoid questions that could deter their prospect from doing business with them. They barrel forward with their rehearsed speech about their product or service rather than having a conversation about what's most important to their prospects. In contrast, servant salespeople care about their prospect's long-term strategies and desires. They want to know all they can about their prospect's thoughts and beliefs so they can best serve that person when the time comes.

None of the salespeople we met at Starlight Palace that day had been trained on these servant selling strategies, and it showed. If you find yourself talking a lot about what you are offering in each of your demonstrations with your prospects, you're probably not selling much.

When it's time to move to the Demonstration step—when it's time to actually talk to someone about your product or service— here's the best advice I can give you: Don't spend much time on it. Seriously. Maybe 5 percent of your time should be spent on the Demonstration. I can describe our coaching services in a couple minutes. Unless it's an incredibly complex process or product (and even the most complicated product or service can be summed up with ease), you can probably describe whatever you sell in a few minutes too.

You'll need to explain your product or service, of course, and answer questions. You'll need to know your stuff. Don't spend too much time on it, though. If you've served your prospect well up to this point, the Demonstration will be the easiest part.

Unfortunately, I see a lot of salespeople making mistakes that can be easily avoided in this step. Let's look at a few of the most common ones.

Mistake #1: Not Getting Permission
You should always get permission when transitioning to talk about your product or service. Don't just jump into it.

Servant salespeople get permission to demonstrate their product because they respect the other person. They don't just launch into what they are offering, since that would come across as selfish. During the Demonstration step, you should be focused on others and what they would like to do. Once you have found a need for what you are offering (during the Introduction step), you owe it to your prospect to figure out whether your products or services will help meet their need.

If I were selling our coaching program, I might ask for the prospect's permission by saying, "Can we talk about coaching now? Is that all right?" Most of the time they say yes. But sometimes they say no, and when they do, you need to honor their answer and not proceed with the sales process. If you've done all the preceding steps well, you will rarely get a no to this question. But when it does happen, the way you react will strongly determine whether your prospect will want to speak with you later about your product.

I usually ask a few more questions to understand why the answer is no. I may say, "I think we figured out that there's a pretty big need here. I don't know if you'd agree. From some of the things you've already told me, it sounds like you believe in accountability and you recognize that there is a lack of it in your life right now. I really think we should talk about coaching. Are you open to chatting about it now?" If the answer is again no, then I thank them for their time. Depending on the situation, sometimes I'll set a time to follow up with them.

But I almost always get a yes. Now the door is open for me to share briefly about what we do. If I'm selling workshops, I might say: "Can I tell you about the details of the workshop so we can get you all set up for one?" Notice that in both instances— selling coaching or workshops—I asked if we or I *can*.

Every salesperson in every industry can ask for permission. If you're selling cars and have connected with a family, learned about their last car, and talked with them to build rapport, don't just let them walk off the lot after establishing their need. Ask for permission to show them your product. Say, "Can we look around the lot together? I've got a few things in mind. You want to start walking?"

Another example is in real estate. You might ask for permission by saying, "Can we jump in the car and look at a few properties?" Or maybe, "Can we take a virtual tour of a few places I know of that might fit your budget?"

If you're a mortgage lender, you might ask, "Would you like for me to do some math and put numbers together for you?" Or maybe, "Do you want to give me some information so I can see what your best interest rate would be?"

By asking for permission to move to the Demonstration, you're keeping the focus on servant selling. You're letting the prospect continue to feel in control and confident about the relationship. That's what you want. If you really care about helping people, the last thing you want is for them to feel pressured or coerced into doing something.

Mistake #2: Talking Too Much

As we discussed in the last chapter, many salespeople think the Demonstration is where the sale gets made. As a result, they often jump to this step too quickly. Then, once they get there, they chatter on and on about their product or service with details the prospect doesn't care about, like Emmie and I experienced at Starlight Palace. Instead of working on improving their relational skills and building rapport, they invest time in studying their product, digging into the details so they can answer every conceivable question.

Unfortunately, sales managers often encourage that mistake. They think product knowledge will convince the prospect to buy. Can I be candid with you? That's just silly. I talk with managers frequently who aren't happy with their sales team's numbers, but they say they have training meetings all the time. When I ask what they talk about in those meetings, it's all about the product or service they offer.

When I ask what they're teaching that will actually help their people sell more, I get crickets.

Managers often misread what their people need and focus too much on the Demonstration step. They give their people detailed product information that doesn't lead to better sales results. I do understand that some products are complicated and require more insight, but product training is rarely going to be the reason anyone buys from you. All the product training in the world can't beat a skilled servant salesperson who does all the preceding steps we've discussed.

In fact, a lot of salespeople lose the sale in this step because they won't stop talking about the product. They talk prospects past the Buying Line, a concept I'll explain more in the next chapter on the Closing step.

Servant sellers understand that people love to buy but hate to feel sold. Closing when someone crosses the Buying Line serves your prospect and allows him or her to buy when they are ready—not too soon and definitely not too late.

Mistake #3: Using I Instead of You and We

I call it making a "you-turn." It applies at every step of the sales cycle, but it's especially evident during the Demonstration step because the tendency is to talk about what you do using "I" instead of "we" language. Many salespeople say, "I do this" or "I do that" instead of "You could benefit from this" or "We can help you do that."

It's a subtle but important distinction. Use language that is inclusive during the Demonstration and throughout the process, keeping the focus on your prospect and how you might work together. When you're talking about your business and what you do, use *us* and *we* so the theme of the conversation continues to be one of sharing. *We* and *us* imply a relationship-rich environment.

Along this same line, make sure you are not the topic of the conversation. Even if you are super successful, resist the urge to talk about yourself. Your prospect does not want to hear about your success. I could give you many examples of "super salespeople" and "marketing gurus" who boast about their success, showing off their yachts and mansions and fancy cars. Their message to prospective clients is, "You can have all this too if you just buy what I'm selling!" That approach is the antithesis of servant selling. The moment the sales process becomes about you, you've lost most people. That's why dropping the references to *I* and using language with *you*, *we*, and *us* is so important.

The 4 Quadrants of Vocal Variety

Although you shouldn't spend too much time on the Demonstration, one thing you should do during this step is liven it up with intentional vocal variety. What do I mean by that? If you've ever seen the television show *The Wonder Years* or the classic film *Ferris Bueller's Day Off*, you may recall the teachers, both played by Ben Stein. Talk about monotone! He intentionally droned on and on so much that no one paid attention. Don't be that person who says good things in such a boring way that you put your prospect to sleep. And don't be the person who talks so fast that your prospect feels like they're being somehow fooled simply because they can't keep up.

When people listen to someone speaking, their emotions are influenced by the volume and rate of the speaker. Just like a DJ can change the way the guests feel at a wedding by playing some crowd favorites, you too can impact the mood of your prospect by introducing a mechanical change in delivery.

There are four quadrants of vocal variety you can use during your Demonstration and throughout the sales cycle. Like most salespeople, you probably have a natural quadrant that you talk in the whole time. Doing this is selfish, though, because it means you're not adjusting for your prospect by looking for ways to keep the Demonstration interesting. You are only doing what's natural or easy for you.

When you shift between the quadrants and use vocal variety, however, you create a natural connection with your customer. This dramatic shift helps keep the listener engaged and feeling what you are feeling.

Understanding these quadrants will help you choose the best volume and rate of speed to fit the moment. Each quadrant accomplishes something different, conveying a different emotion. This simple 2 x 2 paradigm shows how volume and rate affect the emotions:

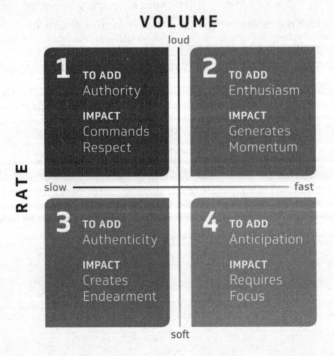

- Quadrant 1: Loud and Slow. To add Authority. *Impact*: Commands Respect.
- Quadrant 2: Loud and Fast. To add Enthusiasm. *Impact:* Generates Enthusiasm.
- Quadrant 3: Soft and Slow. To add Authenticity. *Impact:* Creates Endearment.
- Quadrant 4: Soft and Fast. To add Anticipation. *Impact:* Requires Focus.

Think of your conversation like an EKG that shows the ups and downs of the rhythm of your heart. Every sales conversation has a rhythm of its own. Great conversationalists don't stay in one quadrant. They bounce all over the place. Servant salespeople do the same thing—especially during the Demonstration step. Some salespeople think that if they speak with excitement the whole time, their prospects will stay excited. But that will only exhaust your prospect. On the other hand, stay monotone for twenty minutes, and your prospect will fall asleep.

If you stay in quadrants 1 and 3, talking loudly all the time, you'll likely make people angry and defensive. If you stay on the other side, in quadrants 2 and 4, you'll stay quieter and make a friend, but you probably won't create a connection that would lead to a sale.

As we discussed in chapter 7, you need to go low and slow during the Approach step because that is your first impression. For the Approach, you want to connect with your prospect and be sure you are making sense so that your prospect isn't skeptical of you. Once you reach the Demonstration, however, you should keep your prospect entertained. Liven up the details of your presentation and the parts that aren't very engaging. Speak fast and in a higher tone of voice to create excitement.

For example, I try to generate excitement when I'm talking about the details of our coaching. Granted, it's not too difficult because I genuinely believe in the power of what we offer. But imagine hearing the following information spoken in a higher volume and faster pace versus a softer, monotone way:

> You take a personality profile assessment. You also do a self-assessment. Then you get assigned to your coach. Your coach has ten-plus years of top-producing sales and sales leadership experience. They're a sales and sales leadership pro. They've done it. They've been in the trenches. You also get videos . . .

One approach produces energy, the other doesn't. I also like using excitement with 3-D names—not only during the Demonstration but throughout the sales cycle—to bring more energy and passion around those quick stories of people who've benefited from my services. When you talk fast but also soft, you create anticipation. This technique is great when you're telling stories as you build up to the conclusion. I softly but quickly say, "And then she did this. Then she did that." It's like I'm telling a secret.

Then you can follow with your solution in a softer but slower pace to establish yourself as an authentic expert. If you're using a 3-D name story, you might say quietly, pausing for effect: "That's why he got a coach . . . to help him with all the pieces of his life . . . that were falling apart."

You can also go soft and slow to authentically highlight the emotional parts of your 3-D name stories: "Bob's at Merrill Lynch here in Nashville. . . . Not only did Bob triple his income when he got into coaching . . . but he now has a relationship with his fourteen-year-old daughter that he didn't have before this program. . . . That's the stuff that makes me happy . . . and that's why I do what I do."

Experiment with the vocal quadrants and see what works best. Remember, you want to serve your prospect, so don't just focus on what feels normal for you. Find the vocal styles that serve your prospect well and help them move toward making the best decisions.

During the Demonstration step, your goal is to present your product or service in a way that will help your customer or fulfill a need. When you've followed the Pre-approach, Approach, and Introduction, the Demonstration will almost be a formality. In the next chapter, we'll cover the second-most important step (the Introduction being the first): Closing.

Putting the Principles into Action

Do you know enough about your product or service to provide a quick and engaging demonstration for your prospect? This part of the process should become second nature to you. If you don't know the details that are relevant to the buyer, he or she won't either. If you don't already have a script prepared for this, do it now!

What is your natural vocal quadrant? What vocal variety could you add into your presentation? Write a brief outline of your presentation and note what vocal quadrant would be appropriate to use in each section.

The chapter lists four common mistakes people make during the Demonstration step: not getting permission, talking too much, skipping the Introduction step, and using *I* instead of *you* and *we*. Of those four mistakes, which one are you most likely to make? How can you work on this to improve your servant selling skills?

Monitor how much you talk during this step of the sales cycle. Video yourself during a mock demonstration or ask someone to listen in or join you on a sales call. Where do you need to tighten your presentation? Are you scripted? Do you need to practice more? Make a game plan and execute it.

CHAPTER 10

CLOSING: ASK FOR THE SALE

To Close Well Is to Serve Well

Before my senior year of high school, the private school I attended shut down due to financial problems and other issues. At that time, I was all about sports, and my coach, Larry Romine, had taught me so much about having a strong work ethic and pursuing excellence, so I followed him to New Life Christian Academy. I confess I did not exactly apply myself academically that year, but I still managed to graduate in the top third of my class. (There were only nine students, but I'll take it!)

One incident during my senior year taught me a lot about selling and life. Elder Greg Jackson was the principal of that small school, and like a lot of leaders in smaller organizations, he filled many different roles. But no matter what he was doing, he always wore a suit!

Elder Jackson taught us about history and culture. He taught us math too, but it came from a real-world perspective because he also had a successful home-based business called Prepaid Legal (now Legal Shield). Unknown to me, he made his living recruiting and selling, so he was always looking for opportunities to teach us what he'd learned from the experience.

Elder Jackson taught us practical information, like the classic Rule of 72 for investing, how business really works, and how to make a profit. But one of the best lessons I learned from him began in his classroom on the very first day of school. He started class by asking, "What do you want to be when you leave here? What do you want to do with your life when you've finished high school and then college?" He told us we weren't in middle school anymore. It was time to get practical.

He went around the room asking each of us what we wanted to do in life. Students offered various responses. Someone said he wanted to be a firefighter. Another said an astronaut. One of my best friends said, "I want to be rich." Being a businessman himself, Elder Jackson seized the teaching opportunity. "Tell me more about that," he said. "How are you going to do that?" He ended up giving a memorable lecture about what being rich means and defined it as enriching other people's lives. "You do that," he said, "and you'll be rich."

Then he asked me. Now, one of my defense mechanisms is to use humor to deflect when I feel pressure. It's a way to keep people at a distance while still seeming fun and engaging. With the conversation focused on me, I didn't know what to say.

Elder Jackson leaned forward and put his hand on the table where I sat. As he did, his watch appeared below his jacket sleeve and shirt cuff. It was a gorgeous watch with a blue face and diamonds all around the rim. "David" he asked, "what do you want to do in life?"

"Elder Jackson," I deflected, "that's a really nice watch."

"Thanks," he replied without shifting his eyes from mine.

"Can I have it?" I asked.

"Yes," he answered. "Now tell me what you want to do with your life."

I don't remember what I said after that. All I remember is that he said yes to my request to have his watch. I'll never forget it.

For the rest of the school year, my friends razzed me about it. "He said he was going to give you that watch, right?" they said. "Well, take him up on his offer. Go get it!" I had just been joking to ease my feelings of awkwardness, but Elder Jackson had said yes. I wondered from time to time, "Should I ask him about it again?"

The chatter kept going all year. Finally, it was graduation day. We didn't just walk across the stage and get our diploma. Because there were only nine people in our senior class, Elder Jackson was able to talk about each of us during the ceremony.

For some reason, he saved me for last. First, he gave me honors for my sports achievements that year and then he thanked me for bringing a spirit of winning to the school. He continued to say complimentary things about me, making me feel like a million bucks.

"David Brown, everybody," Elder Jackson announced as he shook my hand to congratulate me one last time. As audience members applauded politely, I turned and began walking off the stage. But he called me back. "David," he said, "there's actually something else I want to say."

I turned around, confused and concerned.

"Do you remember the first day I met you in class and the first question I asked you?"

"Yes, of course," I responded nervously, wondering where he was going with this. Would he ask me to give a speech about it then and there?

"Do you remember what you asked me that day?"

"Yes, sir, I do. I asked if I could have your watch." I noticed then that he had it on, just like always.

Elder Jackson started to take it off. "I'm not going to give you a speech about how you need to be on time in the next chapter of your life or anything like that. What I want to teach you—in fact, what I want to teach all of you," Elder Jackson said, pausing to look at the rest of the students, "is an important life lesson. As you move forward in your life, you need to ask for what you want."

He handed the watch to me and quoted a verse from the Bible where Jesus says, "Ask and it shall be given to you." He continued, "David, the only reason you're getting this watch is because you asked for it. I've been working with people, families, and businesses all my life, and I've seen that people who don't ask for what they want miss out on so much. There are many times in your life that you will ask and you'll hear no. Keep asking. Ask for what you want."

The watch was too big for me when I put it on my wrist, so I had a few links taken out. It was on my wrist every summer as I went selling door-to-door. I heard *no* countless times, but I kept knocking and asking. And every time I looked at that watch, I heard those powerful words: "Keep asking. Ask for what you want."

Elder Jackson probably didn't realize it at the time, but he had taught me one of the most important lessons in selling (and in life): always ask for what you want.

Why Don't We Ask?

How about you? Do you ask for what you want in life every single time you want something?

Be honest.

I often ask this question when I'm speaking to groups of salespeople. Almost always, a handful of people will insist they do, but the overwhelming majority say no, they don't always ask for what they want. And these are people who make a living by asking for a sale!

Why don't more of us follow Elder Jackson's advice and ask for what we want? I have a few theories. For one, maybe we don't feel like we deserve to get what we want. Maybe we carry baggage from childhood or life experiences that convince us we're not good enough. Maybe we've been told by significant people in our lives that we're not worthy, and we've played that script in our heads so many times that we begin to believe it at a subconscious level.

Maybe we were taught not to ask. Walk through the grocery store and you'll hear little kids constantly asking their parents for stuff. What do their parents usually say? "No! Stop asking. Don't ask me again!" Many of us were taught unintentionally from an early age not to ask for what we want.

That's why with our own young children, Emmie and I have tried to respond to their questions in a way that encourages them to keep asking, even if the answer is no. We don't indulge our kids' every request, but we also don't want them to be afraid to ask for what they want. "No, you can't have a candy bar, but thank you for asking," we might say. "No, you're not getting that toy, but thank you for asking."

Another reason we don't ask for what we want is that we're simply afraid of being told no. No one likes rejection. We tend to take it personally rather than seeing it as part of the sales process. Remember, if we have a No Goal, we *want* to hear that word. But if we're afraid of hearing no, we may feel like it's easier not to ask.

We also might not ask because we're worried about looking pushy, or because we believe that if we do a good job for our clients, they will give us referrals without us having to ask. Finally, we simply may not know how to ask. Maybe we've never been trained in how to close. Or maybe we see Closing as a bad thing, a negative but required step in the sales process. Closing isn't negative. It is simply helping someone move to the point of decision—helping them determine whether the product or service is going to help fulfill their need. Closing well is serving well.

The Strike Out Principle

What's the worst that can happen when you ask for the sale? You strike out. There is no shame in striking out, though. The best salespeople strike out most of the time. Sales is a numbers game. The question is not *if* you strike out. That's a given. The question is, *when* you strike out, will you strike out swinging?

Baseball is one sport I didn't play much, but when I did play, I knew there was a difference between striking out looking and striking out swinging. When you strike out looking, the bat never moves. You let the pitch go by and do nothing. It even gets recorded on the scorecard as a backward "K" to record the fact that you didn't even swing at the pitch.

But when you strike out swinging, you have shown that you tried. Your buddies in the dugout don't make fun of you when you at least try to hit the ball. They say, "Good try. That's all right—you gave it a shot." If you strike out looking, though, that's a different story. No one is impressed by someone who watches the ball go by, and your teammates might let you know it.

At Southwestern Consulting, we call it the Strike Out Principle: *always take the swing.* The greatest mistake a salesperson can make at this stage of the sales cycle is not taking the swing. Yet I see it happen all the time during the Closing step. Sincere salespeople will put tons of effort into the sales conversation. They will do all the hard work and bring the conversation right up to the closing and then simply not ask for the sale.

This is doing a massive disservice to your prospects. As a servant salesperson, you want to honor your prospects by asking for the sale directly, without any vagueness or confusion. When you use imprecise language at the Closing step, it only creates indecision, and you may not get a straight answer. Servant salespeople care about their prospects by asking them, clearly and concisely, to buy what they are selling. Asking for the sale takes away any stress or stagnancy, and you know how to follow up if needed.

In service to your prospect, you need to get practical and move the sale forward by closing. Depending on what you're selling, start filling out the enrollment form or paperwork. Ask for credit card information. Then you can get a legitimate and straight yes or no.

Ironically, many salespeople back off at this point because they don't want to pressure the prospect. But the reality is that if you don't ask for the sale, all the pressure is on the prospect to make the next move. Servant selling is about relieving pressure, not creating more. Most people naturally back off when pressured, which makes you less likely to get the sale if you're indirect. But if you've established the right buying atmosphere, people won't complain when you ask for the sale because you're not putting any pressure on them when you ask them clearly.

Of course, sometimes no matter what you do, you're going to get somebody who just decides to be difficult that day. How do you handle that during the Closing step? Persist with enthusiasm.

Even when someone is negative and tells me they would never do a workshop with me, I say, "Great. You said you do your team meetings on Tuesday. Which Tuesday do you want me to come out?" The person might say, "I told you, Dave, you're not coming out." Then I'll move on, but not without asking them to buy. I'm at least going to swing the bat—with a smile!

Don't worry, you aren't being pushy. When you close the right way, with a servant's heart, you are simply guiding your prospect through the process. You want to make sure they have enough information about what is being sold. I have learned through experience that people will say no before they are fully aware of what you are asking. Make sure you have done "the ask." Otherwise, it's a wasted interaction, and that doesn't serve anyone well.

If, for some reason, the prospect is very resistant and won't let me get to the Introduction or anywhere near the Demonstration (let alone move to the Closing step), I might say, "The coaching program takes this long, it costs this much, and it will change your life. Do you want to do it?" This last-ditch effort is another way to swing the bat. The truth is, if you don't even try to close the sale, why are you there? It's crucial to finish what you started and complete the sales cycle.

When you've followed all the servant selling principles to this point, the most respectful thing you can do is ask for the sale whether you feel like the prospect is with you or not. That way, they can either buy from you or move on, without any confusion as to what your intentions were. Striking out swinging gives you credibility as a salesperson. It also gets you a clear yes or a clear no, which relieves your prospects... and you.

Closing Consciousness

The familiar axiom reminds us that "timing is everything." When you are a servant seller, you want to know when the time is right to close. To do that, you can use trial closes along the way to get your prospect comfortable with saying yes so that they can overcome their natural resistance to change.

For those unfamiliar, a trial close is a series of questions used throughout your sales conversation to assess your prospect's readiness to make a buying decision. These questions create a clearing for positive responses on minor connection points. Trial closing is a big part of servant selling because you are gauging your prospect's level of interest along the way. If the responses are positive, you stay the course. And if the responses are negative, then you'll want to get to the *no* faster so you can avoid being in the *maybe* category. It's the best way to truly honor someone's time.

In the last chapter, we saw how important it is to avoid talking too much during the Demonstration step. You need to know when to move to a close so that you don't talk people past their Buying Line. What's the Buying Line? Every conversation has one. Over the course of the presentation, it will emerge. If you close too early, then you won't get the sale; if you close too late, you won't get the sale either.

Think about a time when a prospect seemed genuinely excited about your product or service, and you were certain they were going to buy. But when you finally pulled out the contract or agreement and went to close, they said, "I need to think about it."

What happened? Why do so many people seem ready to buy and then end up not buying? Much of the time, it boils down to overselling. That's why understanding the Buying Line is extremely important.

If you've done your job during the sales cycle, you've identified the need. Your prospect knows what the product is and wants
it. It's time to close. Unfortunately, a lot of salespeople make the
mistake of talking past that point. They go on and on about the
product or service without asking for the sale: "Oh, let me show
you this next section. You're going to love this feature too."

Eventually, the more you talk, the more your prospect will
begin rethinking their decision to buy. *Maybe I'm making the
wrong decision*, they think. They get cold feet and back out, all
because you didn't serve them well when you continued to talk
instead of close.

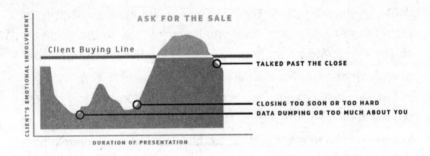

How are you supposed to know a customer has crossed over
the Buying Line and into the zone above? Just like a good poker
player reads his or her opponent's "tells," a servant seller knows to
look for the customer's buying signs. Once you see more than one
of these buying signs, it is time to stop presenting and start closing.

Sometimes a physical cue alerts you. Maybe they're nodding
their head with you or they're starting to fill out the paperwork.
Sometimes it's a verbal cue. They might be agreeing with you,
saying, "Yeah, yeah, yeah," or "Hmm ... mm-hmm." Additionally,
you know it's time to close when your prospect is:

- Asking lots of questions.
- Laughing and giggling a lot.

- Carrying a wallet or checkbook.
- Touching their significant other, if present.
- Looking at the product closely for a second time.
- Reading the paperwork intently.
- Offering long, personal responses to open-ended questions.

This hypothetical Buying Line exists in every conversation. If you've done your Introduction and Demonstration the right way, the Closing is the next step.

Take that step.

Serve When You Close

People are wired differently. That's not news, but it's easy to forget when you're ready to close a sale. Under stress, you'll default to your natural personality wiring and do what feels comfortable. But what if your prospect isn't wired like you?

I have asked to borrow an insightful concept presented in the book *Navigate 2.0: Selling the Way People Like to Buy*. The premise is that there are four basic buying and selling styles every salesperson should be aware of: Fighter, Entertainer, Detective, and Counselor.[9]

The Fighter. When I engage a Fighter personality in a potential buyer—someone who isn't afraid to ask challenging questions—I know they want to quickly understand the bottom line. They want clear choices and like to feel in control. A good close for a Fighter would be the Choice of Two Positives: "How do you want to get started? Do you want to use a credit card? Do you want to put it through your bank account?" They pick. They're in control.

The Entertainer. Entertainers love imagining all the cool things they could do with your product or service. They enjoy telling stories and want to know how buying will help them tell even better stories. With Entertainers, the Crystal Ball Close is magical. For example, if I were closing an Entertainer about our coaching services, I might say:

> Okay, hypothetically, Chantelle, let's say we had a crystal ball here. I know it seems quirky but stay with me. Six months down the road, your business is blowing up, you've got the right people in the right seats, and you are more specific on doing the things that you want to do. You and your coach would build all of this.
>
> Looking at all this, six months down the road, how good would you feel as a business owner if these things were in place? How good would that make you feel? That's why you do it. That's why you get a coach. We're going to help you with every one of those things and make them a reality.

Entertainers love imagining a bigger, better tomorrow and playing with what could be.

The Detective. On the other hand, Detectives are analytical. They're your architects and planners. They ask a bunch of questions. They don't want stories to fuel the imagination; they want the facts and data to make logical decisions. To serve Detectives well, I use the Product, Performance, and Price Close. With this close, you repeat everything you talked about. You talk about the product, performance, and price again. Then you ask, "Does that make sense to you?" Detectives love it when everything makes sense! If the answer is yes, you say, "Great. Let's get started!"

The Counselor. Counselors are all about the team. They move more slowly and make methodical decisions, often including others. Unlike Fighters, they do not respond well to being asked to make a quick choice. They need to proceed cautiously and think about how the decision affects others. I've found the best close to use with these people is the Walk-Out Close. If I'm in person, I might say: "I'm going to step outside for a minute to respond to a text. You guys talk about it. I'll be right back." Or, "I've got to check in with my wife. She called while we were talking. Take a little time to talk it over."

If I'm closing on the phone and can't do the Walk-Out Close, I might say, "Hey, I know it's really important to you to get with the right people and ask them what they think. Can we talk tomorrow? What's the best time to follow up?"

Counselors want space to process their decision and check with other people—even if it's just with their dog. When you give them space to think things through, you are selling to Counselors in the way they want to be sold.

As a servant seller, you need to figure out your prospect's buying style as you go through the sales cycle—especially when you get to the Closing step. It all begins with knowing your own selling style and how that affects your default approach to sales. For example, I'm a Fighter, so my default close is to assume someone will make a choice and buy. If I didn't understand the different buying styles, I would probably say each time, "Let's just get you started!" But it's not about me, or at least it shouldn't be in the servant selling process.

Servant sellers care enough to learn about their prospect's personality and needs. They use the information they have gathered—because they have truly listened to their prospect— to craft a unique closing technique that makes their prospect feel comfortable.

What's in Your Closing Toolbox?

When it comes to mastering the practical magic of Closing, it's important to remember that closing is a process, not a one-time event. Just like a professional golfer doesn't only use one club, servant sellers don't only use one close. You need to have multiple closes memorized and ready to use for different situations and personality styles.

Make sure you're reinforcing a buying atmosphere along the way, especially as you move to the Closing. The servant selling approach takes the pressure off the prospect and frees them to make the best decision. You can say, "This may not be a fit for you—and that's totally fine, but . . ." If your product or service is not a fit for them, you can make the ask (remember, strike out swinging!) and then skip right to the referral step when they say no.

Understand that it takes several closes to help someone make a decision. This is critical to becoming a servant salesperson because you want to focus on finishing well. I estimate that the average salesperson has two closes they turn to again and again. A lot of people use a simple open-ended, noncommittal close like "How does it sound?" or an assumptive close like "Go ahead and sign here." But having just two closes is like trying to fix a car with only a hammer and screwdriver. You need more closing tools in your toolbox if you're going to serve and sell more.

Closing Techniques to Master

Successful salespeople have at least five closes they've mastered. By having many closing techniques to choose from, you'll be able to connect with your prospect more effectively and move the process along efficiently, serving your prospects well.

Here's an easy reference guide to the most effective closing techniques to put in your servant selling toolbox. Some of these closes are adapted from the different ways to sell to the four personality types described earlier in the chapter.

The Self-Close

This technique is simple. Just ask the prospect, "Why is [product or service] important to you?" For example, if I'm talking about coaching, I'd say, "So, Betsy, why is coaching so important to you?"

After your prospect essentially tells you why they should buy your product or service, invite them to make a decision, perhaps with an Assumptive Close. You can say, "Let's get you signed up." "Let's schedule it." "Get your credit card and let's get started."

The Agreement Close

Ask leading questions with agreements attached. You want to encourage the prospect to nod along with you and eliminate any remaining barriers to making a decision. Consider questions like these:

"If I'm reading you right, it seems like you think this is a good idea, right?"

"Looks like a winner, doesn't it?"

"This would be super beneficial, wouldn't it?"

"This could save you a massive amount of time, couldn't it?"

"This should be a no-brainer, shouldn't it?"

The Choice of Two Positives Close

This is best used with someone who wants to be in charge and has a strong personality, like the Fighter we described before. It provides choices, allowing the person to focus on how they want to get started. You might ask questions that give options:

"What works better for you, Monday or Tuesday?"

"Would you rather meet at your office or a coffee shop?"

"Would you rather pursue [Program A] or [Program B]?"

The Crystal Ball Close

As mentioned earlier, this approach puts your prospect as the main character in their story and envisions what the future could look like with your product or service. This works well with people who enjoy storytelling, like Entertainers. With this close, you might say something like, "Visualize yourself five years from now enjoying the [product/service]. What would it feel like to enjoy the benefits we've been discussing? Let's make this a reality for you!"

The Takeaway Close

Sometimes called the Pullback Close, this technique works well if you've created the right buying atmosphere: "Our [product/service] is the best, but it's not for everyone. Just like a BMW or Tesla is not for everyone, this might not be a fit for you."

This technique gets people to reveal their objections. It triggers a Fear of Missing Out (FOMO) and employs psychology. People often want what they can't have, so if you move to take the option away, it can encourage someone to finally act.

The Product, Price, Performance Close (PPP)

This is a great close to use for prospects who love to research and ask questions, like Detectives. The PPP Close is all about rehearsing the core details using the words *price, product,* and *performance* and then closing with a logical, direct statement.

Product: "Do you think the [product/service] is something you will use?"

Price: "Do you think, based on the [value] you're receiving, that the investment is fair?"

Performance: "Based on our conversation so far, do you believe I will follow through on the customer service and deliver on what we've discussed?" (In other words, do you trust me?)

Direct Closing Statements:

"You need to do this."

"This is logical."

"This is a no-brainer."

"There's nothing else to think about."

"You will be glad you made a decision to do this."

The If/Then Close
"If we can do _____ , _____, and _____ , then will you be willing to move forward today?"

The 1–10 Close
"On a scale of 1–10, with 10 being 'sign me up right now' and 1 being 'I'm not interested at all,' where are you? Tell me why you are at number __ and not at number __? What would it take to get you to a 10?"

The Yes Question Close
"Based on what you've been telling me, this is what you wanted, right?"

The Impending Event Close
"In order to get this delivered by [date], we'll need to get started today."

T-Bar or Ben Franklin Close

This technique works best when you can show someone visually, either on paper or on-screen, two lists side by side showing both the pros and cons about the decision. Just make sure the positives outweigh the negatives.

The No Really Means Yes Close

Use reverse psychology with this question: "Is there any reason why we shouldn't move forward today?"

The Boomerang Question

Redirect the question, "So how much is it?" by saying, "Well, it depends. What are you paying currently?" Answer the question with a question and then go back to your presentation or closing process.

The Walk-Out Close

This technique works for someone leading a team or in any group sales setting where a consensus is needed. Counselor personalities also respond well to this close. There are essentially five steps:

Plant positive seeds. Get the group talking about what they like best. Look at a couple of the influencers and ask, "Charlie, what is your favorite part about our [product/service]?" or "Melissa, you seem to be excited about it. What is your favorite part?"

Ask for the exit. "Keisha, I know you're a wise decision-maker and would want to discuss this with your team before making a final decision." Stand up and pull out your phone. "I have a few emails to check and will give you all time to talk without me in the room to make sure you are on the same page."

Ask for the answer today. With your hand on the door handle as you're leaving, ask: "By the way, we have discussed everything you need to know to make a decision. Now it's just up to you guys to decide if you want to move forward or not. As we discussed earlier, either way is fine by me. The only favor I ask is that when I come back in you give me a yes or a no. Does that sound fair?"

Pray. I write this jokingly, but here's the reality: You want to get a yes or a no when you walk back into the room. You want to successfully eliminate the deadly maybe. So, if you're like me, you might send up a quick prayer!

Reenter and close. Use an Assumptive Close when you return, giving them space to answer the questions: "Would you rather start today or tomorrow?" "Would you rather pay with a check or a credit card?"

Pull out the contract and ask, "Where do you get your mail, at a PO box or the office?" Place your pen on the contract and look at it until they start filling it out.

At first glance, an Assumptive Close might not seem like something a servant seller would use, but when you use this technique, you give your prospects space to answer questions and the ability to give you a direct yes or no. That's service!

Servant salespeople love the Closing step because they like to help their prospects make a decision one way or the other. As I mentioned, leaving someone in a state of indecision is one of the highest forms of disservice. Your prospect will appreciate your directness when closing. When you ask clear questions, you will get clear answers. And when you close the right way, you will successfully help someone get from point A to point B in the easiest, wisest, and most respectful way possible.

Putting the Principles into Action

Identify whether your prospect is a Fighter, Entertainer, Detective, or Counselor personality. Understanding your prospect and engaging with them in the way that makes them most comfortable is at the heart of servant selling. Once you've determined their personality type, craft a plan to close the deal accordingly. This will serve your prospect well.

Evaluate your current closing process. Do you always make the ask? How often do you strike out looking versus swinging? Don't give up before your prospect knows what you're offering. Ask yourself whether the last few people who said no knew what you were selling and doing. How could you have closed differently?

Review the closing techniques. Which one will you add to your toolbox? Schedule time right now to practice it so you can use it well.

Video yourself closing a sale during a practice demonstration. Look for what closes you used and if you were clear and concise in your ask for the business. Then, if possible, watch it with your manager and ask for feedback.

CHAPTER 11

DEALING WITH DOUBTS: PERSIST WITH PASSION

Doubts Are Common and Resistance Is Normal

Doubts. Every salesperson hears them when trying to close. Some people call them objections, but calling them objections makes it sound like they are something to overcome, conquer, fight against, and hopefully, eventually defeat. That sounds like win/lose language to me.

Servant sellers don't think that way; instead, they look for win/win opportunities. They care about the person on the other end of the transaction. That's why I prefer to use the word *doubts* instead of *objections*. After all, doubts are normal. Everyone has them, no matter what they are being sold. You can't avoid doubts, but you can prepare for them.

I have encountered many people with doubts in my sales life. In fact, the greatest "sale" I ever made required me to deal with serious doubts. I heard these concerns over a couple of years as I was selling Emmie on the idea of dating me. Believe me, Emmie had plenty of doubts—for good reason—and she wasn't afraid to share them. Whenever I would bring up the topic of dating, she was ready with reasons to say no. I felt like Sam-I-Am at times, hearing no but still persisting with enthusiasm.

When I first met Emmie on a trip for top sales performers, I was a cocky, promising salesperson who had not yet chosen to be a servant salesperson. Add in a little "liquid confidence," and I made an absolute donkey of myself. Worse yet, I had dated a few members of Emmie's team, and I'd acted flaky. Emmie had been their shoulder to cry on. Ugh.

I was sincere as I tried to persuade her to date me. But she had serious doubts about me. Still, I kept trying to convince her. I told her . . .

"I'm a good man. Give me a chance!"

"I'll be the best decision you'll ever make."

"The current Dave is much wiser and more reliable than the previous Dave."

"I want you to be happy."

Initially she flat-out refused to consider me as an option. Memorably, she said, "I would never, ever date you." We were working well together and building a great company because we were an awesome team. When it came to the personal side, though, she was very clear—no way.

I was undeterred. For me, a no just meant I was getting a response and making progress. Somehow, I managed to convince her to join me and my family for one Thanksgiving, and we had a wonderful time. But the next two months were awkward. She was casually dating other guys, and I just couldn't get her out of my mind.

I finally persuaded her to go on a trial date. I promised it would be informal and fun, nothing serious. It went great. The following week was Valentine's Day, and even though I had initially promised to keep things casual, I knew I was falling in love. I told her, "I can't take this. I'll either be your boyfriend, or I'll accept that the answer is forever going to be no. Please let me know by 5:00 p.m. on Friday."

It was an agonizing week, especially since we worked in the same office. Emmie spent every free minute asking her friends and family for advice about what to do, and I had no idea what her answer was going to be. On Friday, a few minutes before 5:00, she came to my office.

"What's your answer?" I asked her.

Every second after that question seemed to take an eternity. Finally, she said, "I'll be your girlfriend."

I was overjoyed! We immediately went down the hall and told our colleagues. None of them seemed the least bit surprised by our big news.

I didn't just address Emmie's doubts one time. I had to sell her numerous times over our years of dating. I confess that I can be a control freak. I'm also stubborn and like to win arguments, and I don't say, "I'm sorry" enough. I knew she had a lot of reasons not to be with me. But I intentionally worked on all my shortcomings, with Emmie's help.

I don't know how Emmie managed to push past all the doubts and move toward marriage. Eventually she did, and we officially started a family. I'm so thankful she chose me and all my flaws.

You probably have your own relationship stories or have had a similar experience where you had to address someone's doubts about you. In both relationships and work, always expect to encounter doubts because resistance is normal.

Programmed to Doubt

As a servant salesperson, you want to get your product or service into the hands of everyone you talk to because you love helping people meet their needs. You believe your product will help your prospects, even when they don't see how yet. Helping people navigate the Dealing with Doubts step is a necessary and important part of showing your prospects how much you care.

Our culture has become so cynical and skeptical about nearly everything that we've become conditioned to say without thinking, "Nope, not interested." It's become an automatic response to object and protest. If you really believe that your product or service can help your prospects, though, you don't quit when you hear no. And if you don't believe in your product, you shouldn't be selling it in the first place!

Why do so many salespeople give up when they hear the first no? It's the same reason the prospect says no—salespeople have doubts too. They doubt their ability to sell. They doubt the quality of their product or service. They doubt many things, so when they hear their prospect's concerns, they simply agree and quit trying. But when they give up, they aren't thinking about what's best for the prospect or about serving them well.

The key to the Dealing with Doubts step is to turn the prospect back to the Cycle of the Sale. Rather than letting doubts distract you from selling, rely on the systems and processes to guide your response.

Remember, as a servant salesperson, you are focused on answering questions and concerns. It's wise to have several responses ready for when you hear certain doubts. My favorite response when I hear any concern is this: "We'll work through that, but start with me on this. Why do you want to do this right now? Why would this be so good for you?" This simple redirect refocuses the person and encourages them to voice their need.

If I'm trying to schedule a meeting, and someone tells me they are busy or asks me to just send them some materials, I redirect with something like this: "Hey, that's actually why I called. I'm just trying to set up a time to . . ."

The word *no* comes in a variety of forms. When somebody says, "I want to think about it," they might be politely saying no. When somebody says, "I need to talk to my [significant other]," they might really mean, "I'm not sold yet." When somebody says, "Send me more information," they actually might be saying, "I don't see enough value to move forward." When someone says, "We can't afford it," they might be thinking, "This is not enough of a priority for me to allocate money toward what you are selling."

In my experience, when someone initially tells me, "No, I am not interested," they haven't learned about my product or service yet. It's our job as servant sellers to understand other people's confusion and clearly communicate how our product or service will benefit them. If they choose to buy, that's great. If they choose not to buy, that's okay too.

When dealing with doubts, don't fence with your prospect and try to persuade them you're right and they are wrong. Even if you win the battle, you'll lose the war.

Doubts don't necessarily mean, "No, I don't want this." They might mean, "I'm not there yet—help me get there." In fact, servant salespeople often must close three to five times before most people clearly understand how a product or service might benefit them.

That's why the Dealing with Doubts step provides such a tremendous opportunity to serve. When people express their doubts or fears, they are inviting you to deliver a solution to their problem.

The Doubt Response Formula

The most common mistake I see salespeople make during the Dealing with Doubts step is directly answering an objection without following a proven formula. That sets up a win/lose dynamic that will keep you from serving your prospect well. Even if they do buy, they'll likely have buyer's remorse because they felt forced to act. Nobody wants that.

You have the opportunity and responsibility to serve your prospect by guiding them through the process to address their concerns. When you follow the Doubt Response Formula, you can focus on serving with persistence and enthusiasm.

Doubt Response Formula

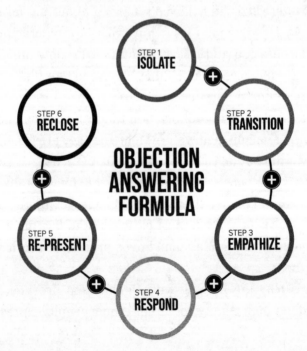

Step 1: Isolate the Doubt

Many salespeople ignore their prospect's doubts. But by isolating the doubt, you are showing that you have heard your prospect and that you care. You are serving your prospect when you spend time getting to the core of their concerns, without distractions.

Address the concerns one at a time to move forward. In this first step, repeat the concern and ask, "Anything else? Did I hear you accurately?" For example, I might say, "Other than [the doubt], is there anything holding you back from moving forward?" Or, "So if it weren't for your concern about [the doubt], you would be ready to get started?"

You'll want to keep repeating this step until you get to the bottom of the true concern. Often you will find that the first doubt is not the real doubt.

By asking the question, you're highlighting the concern. Now you know your goal. Now you know what problem needs to be solved.

If the person gives you two or three concerns, you can still isolate their doubts, but you have to address each one separately. You can't work through two or three doubts at a time because it leaves you with too many moving targets.

Step 2: Use a Transition Statement

It's okay to empathize with someone when they are having doubts. Just make sure you never agree with the doubt itself. Most concerns are excuses that people give to delay moving forward. When you use a transition statement, you are acknowledging their feelings but not agreeing with their doubt.

You might say, "I can understand how you feel" or "I can appreciate that" or "It's understandable at first glance why you might feel that way."

Step 3: Give an Empathy Story
As we often say at Southwestern Consulting, "Everyone suffers from a disease called 'terminal uniqueness.'" Everyone thinks his or her situation and concern is special. Most of the time, it's not.

The best way to eliminate someone's terminal uniqueness is to let them know that a lot of other people have felt the same way. Think back to the list of 3-D name stories you created after reading chapter 7. You can say that you know someone who felt the same way or said the same things but ended up moving forward and working with you anyway! For example, you might tell your prospect, "A client I worked with last month, Jim at [XYZ Enterprises], was also feeling like he didn't have enough money for coaching. But then he said, 'If I can't afford this, I probably *should* do it. Not having a coach might be why I'm not successful enough.'"

Step 4: Respond
The worst way to respond to someone's doubts is to give your opinion of what they should do. The second worst way is to directly answer someone's concerns and try to convince them why they shouldn't have doubts. Ignoring or glossing over your prospect's concerns is not a service-oriented approach.

Continue the 3-D story by saying, "Jim signed up for coaching and had the best quarter of his career. He's currently on track to beat his own sales record. With coaching, you could do the same—and after all we've talked about today, I feel confident that you will."

In this step of the Doubt Response Formula, you are connecting the 3-D story with the person who is sitting in front of you or on the other end of the line. Let the story respond for you. I like to share two or three stories each time to let the prospect know that it's normal to have concerns. I reiterate that people who had similar doubts moved forward and were glad they did.

Step 5: Re-Present
After you respond, re-present the information, or ask another question. I've found that most people voice three to five doubts before they make a decision. This means that you need to be prepared with three to five different answers to their concerns as well as three to five different new selling points to reengage your prospect and get them over the Buying Line.

You may want to ask another question about their needs or wants, which you discussed earlier during the Introduction step. Or you could show another powerful feature of your product or service to add greater value. Review your Demonstration with your manager or peers to identify high-value topics to revisit or focus on here.

Step 6: Re-Close
Don't forget the Strike Out Principle we discussed in chapter 10. Keep swinging! After you've successfully taken your prospect back over the Buying Line, re-close. When selling our coaching to a Realtor, for example, I might say, "You're going to make all that investment back. You're going to make half of that back when you close one house, and we're going to help you close 25 percent more houses than you did last year. Last year you sold ten houses? This year it's going to be at least three more. Let's go ahead and get you started."

I've had a ton of conversations where people go back and forth and tell me they want to think about it. When that occurs,

I might re-close by asking, "If you don't do this, what's going to happen?"

What do they say? "Nothing."

"Well, this route is a whole lot better than nothing, isn't it?" I point out.

Don't be frustrated if it takes a few tries. Be ready to apply a variety of closing techniques, and you'll get a clear answer. Don't leave until you've given it plenty of good swings. Keep working to find the need, and then fulfill it so that you're serving well.

The Four Ps

Most doubts can be sorted into four primary categories. Even though the concerns might sound different when various prospects say them, they really come down to these four real doubts:

PRICE: "I can't afford this."

PROCRASTINATION: "I'd like to think about it."

PURCHASER: "I need to talk this over with . . ."

PROVIDER: "I'm happy with what I'm using now."

The best way to address these doubts is to do so before they come up. For example, you can proactively respond to the procrastination and purchaser concerns during the Introduction step. You can also mention one of the most common doubts you hear and use the answer to the doubt as a selling point during the Demonstration step.

Over the years, I've developed specific responses to each of the P concerns by using evidence of how others solved those problems. Servant salespeople love using stories with each of these Ps because it verifies all they have said about their product as an excellent solution or asset. Using the Four Ps also keeps the focus on your prospects, helping them to feel understood and assured that their concerns will be resolved.

Price

Salespeople usually hear this objection because they have not demonstrated enough value for the price. Once the value exceeds the price, the sale gets made almost every time.

I always follow the Doubt Response Formula when I'm dealing with doubts. My first move is to isolate the concern about money. "If you had the money for it, you'd do this, right? Okay, good. Let's figure it out. Is it just a matter of splitting up payments or stretching them out a little bit differently? Because it sounds like you want to do this, but it's just a matter of figuring it out how to make this work."

Then I get creative about how to make it happen for them. Remember, my focus is on serving my prospect, and I want to help address the need we have uncovered. I continue, "Do you think that could work for you? Great. I'll write down the information while you grab your credit card. What credit card would you like to put it on? Or would you rather take it through your bank account?" Steer the prospect back to the point of commitment once you have worked through the price/money issue. Again, letting your prospect grapple with indecision does not serve them well.

Another reason the price comes up is because it makes many salespeople give up. Most people can relate to feeling like they don't have enough money. As a servant salesperson, however, you can empathize with your prospects but not agree with their doubts. Sometimes, I gently challenge people by saying: "How long have you been telling yourself you can't afford the things you want? The way you're talking right now, you're never going to have the money for the things you want."

When you hear this doubt, realize that it's usually not about the money. People can almost always find the money. I dealt with this doubt when I worked with Taylor Thigpen. Taylor was a new district sales coordinator with Aflac when I met him. He had no money. Zero. But he knew he needed coaching help because so many people had held his position previously and then left the company because they didn't earn enough income. Taylor had many doubts about investing in coaching. We sat and talked for a long time, dealing with doubt after doubt. I talked with him about the many people we had coached and helped reach a new level of success. There was no manipulation, no coercion—I simply told him true stories. And he found a way to pay for coaching.

Two months later, Taylor wasn't making the kind of money he needed to make. I knew he could meet his goals, though, so at the end of June, I told him, "Taylor, you could make $10,000 in July if you did all the things that your coach is telling you to do. Double down and tell yourself, 'No matter what, I'm making $10,000 this month.' And you will make $10,000! Your coach can get you there. You have to trust the process and do everything he says."

Taylor made $11,000 the following month, and he's still one of our coaching clients several years later. At times, he led the entire Aflac team of 16,000 reps and 2,000 managers in various sales and leadership categories. He has been promoted and has become one of the best regional sales coordinators in the state of Tennessee.

There's always a way to serve, even if it takes a little creativity to find out what works best for the client.

Procrastination

"I'm gonna think about it."

Who hasn't heard that response before? When a prospect procrastinates, you must dig in and figure out what piece they're stuck on. Is it their natural inclination to put things off? Did their dad tell them to always get three quotes before making a decision? Is it a rule they've put in place or did somebody in their family advise them to sleep on it?

Again, I isolate the doubt: "So that's the only thing holding you back?" I might add, "Do you need more information to make an educated decision?" If they are a Counselor personality, I sometimes say, "Do you need to talk with someone else before you can make a decision?"

I let the person talk, listening carefully, and then I respond by saying, "I totally appreciate that. Let me ask you this—what's going to change? You say you want to do this, and you say it's going to be good for you. What's going to change by waiting? Just so I'm clear on this, based on the past, are you more likely to do it or not do it by waiting?"

I like to be direct. I've found it is the best way to honor and serve my prospects. After I've done everything I can to answer the concern, I say, "I believe you need to act. Don't wait. You're as close right now to doing this for yourself as you will ever be. Let's do it."

Purchaser

By the time you've reached the Dealing with Doubts step, you should know if your prospect can make the decision to purchase. Otherwise, you'll have to close by setting up an appointment where all the decision-makers can be present. It's better to find out earlier in the sales cycle.

I'm always looking for clues about who else needs to be involved in the decision-making process. Before I get too deep into the conversation, I try to find out who the purchaser is. If anybody else needs to be included, I figure out an indirect way to do that quickly.

Provider

"Thanks, but I'm happy with what I'm using now."

There's a good chance you'll hear this doubt earlier in the process as you begin the Demonstration. The best response here is to go back to the CLASP method I described in chapter 8.

"Sweet," I usually respond. "What do you currently like about them?"

When they tell me what they like, I say, "That's great. If you could, what would you change?"

Then, paint the picture of the new scenario. Tell a story about someone who said they were happy with their current provider and then changed. Then tell another story. I've memorized stories of people to use for every one of these Ps = price, procrastination, purchaser, and provider.

Use those stories to respond to concerns as you go through the Dealing with Doubts step of the sales cycle. Let the stories of all the people you have served with your product or service do the talking for you. It is powerful and humbling to serve people by helping them work through their doubts, fears, and confusion.

Putting the Principles into Action

Make a list of the most common doubts you hear when closing. Next to each of them, write the five best answers to those concerns. Then think of real-life stories of people who have expressed those same doubts and ended up purchasing your product/service anyway. Put their names and a brief note next to the specific doubt so you have a collection of stories on standby.

Prepare three to five different answers to the most common concerns you encounter during the Dealing with Doubts step. Then write down three to five new selling points that you can use to reengage your prospect and get them back over the Buying Line.

Are you ready when you hear the four Ps? How would you respond to each of them? Prepare your script now so you can focus on helping your prospect through the process.

CHAPTER 12

GETTING REFERRALS: ALWAYS ASK

Servant Selling Means Looking for More People to Help

One of my coaching clients, Bob, was starting his new career with all the excitement and enthusiasm in the world. He loved the product he was selling and the people he worked alongside. He was determined to be successful. But during his first few weeks, he couldn't seem to get any momentum. He struggled to get people on the phone, and once he did, they were short with him. When he finally set an appointment to give the demonstration, the prospect never arrived, or they called at the last minute to cancel.

Bob was doing every piece of the sales cycle right. He looked up potential leads and did Pre-approach research. He always had enough people to call because he set a weekly goal of getting ten qualified leads to add to his database. When he called his prospects, he used his scripts/talk tracks and left proper voice mails. His biggest frustration point came two months into his career change, when he was about halfway through his goal for the week of getting ten qualified leads.

During our coaching call, he said in exasperation, "I don't know why I'm even spending my time getting these new names to call! They are going to do what everyone else does and hang up on me, or tell me to call them back later, or cancel an appointment we set up. This sucks! I want this to work out because I love working here, but I can't take this anymore. I might need to do something else."

I just listened, letting him get it all out. Then I asked him how many referrals he got that week, and he said zero. Then I asked how many he got the previous week, and he said zero. Finally, he said, "I don't have anyone to ask for referrals because no one has bought anything from me!"

I responded, "Bob, have you been talking to humans?"

"Of course!" he said. "Tons of humans!"

"That's good," I told him. "Ask everyone you speak with for referrals, especially the ones who say no to you."

He didn't understand. He asked why someone would give him referrals when they didn't want what he was selling.

"Because you asked," I said. "It may not be a fit for the people who said no, but they probably know of someone who does want what you're selling. You'll never know unless you ask."

When I followed up with Bob a few days later, he said he had taken my words to heart. He told me a story about a prospect who had said no to him. Rather than ending the conversation, Bob asked for referrals in a polite and confident way. The person said, "Wow! Even after I told you no, you still asked for others to call on. Let's get together. I want to take a closer look at what you're doing, and I'll make sure to think of other people too." Bob used this proactive approach with lots of people, getting numerous referrals.

When we spoke a few weeks later, he sounded ecstatic. "Suddenly, I love this new career path! I just ask prospects for someone else to call, no matter how they have responded to my demonstration. And then I shut up and write down the names they give me. It works!"

As Bob came to understand, there's no harm (and lots of help) in asking every person you talk to for the name of someone else you might approach with your product or service. That's not being pushy—that's being a servant salesperson, because you are helping to meet needs.

Although every industry is different, the same principles apply during the Getting Referrals step. For example, if you are in car sales, you can call people who have bought from you and ask for referrals. All car dealerships have a database with everybody who has purchased a car from them. They're often called orphaned accounts, and they include people who bought cars years ago. It's not the warmest list, like the guy who bought from you a week ago, but it's a place to start.

If you are in a sales or prospecting slump, chances are it's not because you're bad at your job or that you're working for the wrong company. It's likely because you don't have enough referrals. You may have a fear of asking or be making some technical mistakes when you ask.

In our coaching practice, we often hear people say, "I don't have time to ask for referrals." When someone tells me that, I reply, "What? Don't you want to save time in the future and bless other people—who are connected to your clients—with your products and services?" When I put it like that, they realize how crazy it is to avoid asking for referrals!

A referral is a time multiplier. It allows you to shortcut the sales process and reach more people. Nothing evaporates call reluctance and turns around sales momentum like gathering a bunch of referrals.

Why Don't We Ask?

Having a servant selling mentality means you're always looking for more people to serve. If you run out of people to serve, then you have run out of people to help.

I invite you to see this final step in the sales cycle not as a destination but as part of a continuation strategy. Instead of looking for a way out once you've closed the sale, look for opportunities to serve more people and reengage the cycle. That's why the Getting Referrals step is critically important to the servant seller. It represents the question that every servant salesperson should ask: Who else can I serve?

When someone gives you referrals, it indicates that you have helped them and served them well. This means they are going to want their friends or contacts to also have the same experience with you. (This makes them look good to their people!) Your clients are just sharing the love and service you provided for them. This is servant selling.

Referrals make selling so much easier. In my experience, business that comes from a referral closes ten times faster than other leads (such as a list of names you've purchased). Why? The relationships accelerate the trust process. Rather than having to do cold or lukewarm prospecting, you can shorten the time needed to engage someone and build rapport through the Introduction. You still need to do the work, but it's a much lighter lift when you engage someone from a referral.

If getting referrals makes so much sense, why don't more salespeople do it?

Fear of Failure. We're all familiar with this fear. It's the same reason we don't take the swing and try to close the sale. But failure isn't anything to be afraid of. Rather than worry about being rejected by a prospect or client, we should fear missing out on the opportunity to make a significant impact in someone's life.

Basketball great Michael Jordan saw failure as part of the winning process. I remember watching his famous commercial where he said, "I've missed over 9,000 shots in my career. I've lost almost 300 games. Twenty-six times I've been trusted to take the game-winning shot and missed. I have failed over and over and over again in my life. And that is why I succeed."

This commercial lit a fire under me as a young man and athlete when it first aired in the late 1990s. I recorded the commercial and watched it over and over—probably sixty times. I noticed how Michael Jordan walked, and I practiced walking the same way he did. I memorized his words, and they gave me the strength to push through rejection in sports and later in my career. Michael Jordan's perspective on failure changed my life.

Don't be afraid to fail when asking for referrals. After all, failure never hurt anyone—it's just part of the process of servant selling.

Rushing the Process. Another reason salespeople don't ask for referrals is they think they don't have enough time. They believe they are too busy to ask for referrals and to follow up on them. But as we saw in chapter 6, Pre-approach, that's just silly. Like Bob discovered, if you don't have warm leads—referrals from people you know or have spoken to—you're not going to be busy for long. Your sales funnel will dry up and leave you with nothing but time on your hands.

Rather than categorizing the request for referrals as a time loss, see the Getting Referrals step as a time multiplier, because that's exactly what it is. It empowers you to be more efficient in your sales process so you can help more people.

Asking for More. Another excuse I've heard is that people don't want to ruin a sale they've already made. They're afraid to come across as needy. They say, "I don't want the person to think they're not enough or that I'm not satisfied." But that's not a rational fear. If you've served your clients well, they will want to share the "gift" of you with the people they know.

I've also heard salespeople say, "If they know about someone else who needs me, they'll call me." But the reality is that no one goes through life with you or your services top of mind, no matter how good you think you are. The ideal time to ask for referrals is when you close the sale. That's the moment you are front and center in your client's mind.

The 7-Step Referral Process

Over the years, I've seen that many salespeople don't know how to ask for referrals. They've simply never been taught the technique. As a result, many of them ask this way: "Do you know anybody who needs this product [or service]?" But that approach stumps most people. For example, imagine I were a Realtor, and I asked you right now, "Do you know anybody who needs to buy a house?" Could you give me a name right away? Probably not.

But what if I asked that question differently? Instead, I could say, "Who do you know in the investment space, who is into rental properties, who is a big-picture thinker always looking for a good deal? Do you know anybody who does investments or rentals or anything like that?" Similarly, you might ask, "Based on who you are and who you know, can you think of someone who would be a good person for me to talk to?"

Now let's dive into the 7-step Referral Process that my Southwestern colleagues and I have used for many years during this stage of the cycle. You can use this process every time someone buys something from you.

Step 1. Use a Transition Statement. Start by thanking the person for their business and then build them up. For example, I might say, "Thank you so much for taking this step. Maybe you can help me in another way." As I said, you can adapt the wording to fit your style and situation. The important thing is to thank them, build them up (be authentic), and intentionally transition the conversation.

Step 2. Clearly Ask for the Referral. Just like when you're closing the sale, you have to actually ask for a referral. But don't say the word *referral*. You can use that language when discussing the sales cycle with your coworkers, but don't use it when asking your customer for names. The word can be off-putting.

Instead, begin the ask by relating with your customer. This script is powerful. I often say, "Like you, I prefer to do business with people who are friends or friends of friends. I'm looking to be introduced to people who might share similar values and beliefs as you."

The goal is to speak with every person who needs to know about who you are and what you are offering. If you've served your clients well, chances are they will be happy to help you. If they decide to provide names, that's great; if not, that is okay too.

Step 3. Paint the Picture. Paint a picture that puts the client in your shoes. Let them know exactly what you're looking for: "If you were me, someone who [insert why you do what you do], who would you talk to next?" This gives the person a feeling of control and engages them in the process.

Step 4. Isolate the Faces. The aim is to help them focus on the faces of the people they know. If you've done the Pre-approach and Introduction steps well, you already know a good deal about your client, so prime the pump. Start broad and identify the person's circle of influence. Then get specific.

You might say, "I'm looking for anyone who [list as many specific criteria as possible]. I know you are involved in your [circle of influence] group. Who are you closest to in that group? Who did you sit next to at the last meeting?"

If someone says, "Let me think about it and get back to you later," simply respond with an assumptive, "I believe that postponing or leaving things hanging doesn't serve either of us well," and move the conversation along. The best thing is to get a yes or no so that you don't waste their time—or yours.

Step 5. Write Down the Referral. Think of asking for the referral as closing a sale, because that's really what it is: you want to serve your clients so well that they will be eager to give you names of other people to help. After you ask the specific questions that I listed, break eye contact (if you're in person or on a video call) and look at your referral pad or sheet of paper while you wait. Do not talk again until the person gives you a name.

Step 6. Ask, "Who Else?" As long as your customer is focused on generating names and faces, ask for more. Get as many as you can. Write down any information they give you as quickly as possible, thank them for sharing the name, and ask for more. You can say, "Thank you so much. This is how I do business, and this helps a lot! Who else might be a good fit to talk to?"

Step 7. Get Your Pre-approach Background Information. Once you've gotten names, circle back to get important data:

What is the decision-maker's first name? What time are they home or in the office? What's their best contact number?

If you can, get some idea of who you're dealing with before you approach the referral. Ask your customer, "Tell me about _____. What kind of person is he/she? Straight to the point, detailed, extroverted?" Then you can craft the best strategy that will position you to better serve that person.

This seven-step technique for getting referrals works. One of our coaching clients, Jennifer Perkins, has been very successful in following these steps. Jennifer now owns a successful real estate investment group, but when I first met her, she was an insurance producer at a local State Farm office. Her biggest objective when signing up for coaching with my team was to get more referrals. She was a single mom at the time who needed to increase her income. With the training and accountability of her coach, Jennifer became better and better at asking for names.

At first, Jennifer had a goal of getting five new referrals per month as an insurance producer, and then that grew to ten, then twenty, then thirty. She kept increasing her goal and continued to hit it month after month. She would ask existing customers for referrals to friends and family, people at the grocery store for who they knew, and anyone she talked to who said no to her. She got so good at asking for referrals that she became one of the most successful producers in the region.

After about four years, Jennifer was able to start her own real estate agency and investment firm. Now Jennifer's thriving business is fully fueled by referrals—so many that she cannot get to all of them. She never stops asking everyone, everywhere for names, and her life has changed dramatically for the better.

The SRE Technique

I've created a simple technique for reengaging with existing customers to generate referrals. Your existing customer base is one of your most valuable resources. If you have helped your customers by practicing the principles of servant selling, give them the chance to reciprocate by providing you with names of others you can bless through your services.

The SRE technique gives you 3-D names that will make great stories to add to your collection. It also provides you with actual names of people who are likely to buy what you sell because they have been referred by someone they know and trust.

Choose a handful of people to call from your existing client base. I do this every year. When you get each customer on the phone, begin with service. After a brief greeting, ask, "How have you felt about the service I have provided for you?" Assuming you delivered a positive experience (and you most likely did if you were focused on servant selling), you're going to get a nice response. A lot of people will give you valuable details about their experience, details you can use later.

They might say something like, "I feel like you care about my family, and I can trust you. That's why I do business with you." You can use that as a testimonial to tell someone else what it's like to do business with you. When you hear something positive, respond with, "Wow! Do you mind if I share that with other people?" You just got an awesome 3-D name story you can use with new prospects.

Then take the second step—remind. Let the person know you're still able and willing to serve. Say, "Thank you again for doing business with me. I just want to remind you that if you ever need anything from me, I'm here for you. Give me a call. Do you still have my personal cell phone number? If you have my email address, can I count on you to reach out if you need anything?

Helping you and all my past clients as much as possible over the years is most important to me. I want to be a resource forever."

Finally, ask if there is anybody else you should be talking to so you can provide the same level of service for them: "While we're on it, is there anybody else I can talk to?" Does this technique always generate referrals? No. Sometimes I only get a story or two from some people. But sometimes I get ten referrals.

Here's an email template you can customize to send as a follow-up after asking for referrals:

Hi Alyssa,

It was so good to see you the other day. Thanks for the names of other people I can potentially help. Would you be able to cut and paste the message below and email it or leave it as a voice mail? That way the people you've referred will have a heads-up when I call. I find it really helps. (Of course, feel free to adapt it or personalize it.)

[EMAIL TO CUT AND PASTE]

I hope you don't mind, but I recently gave your contact information to [name, company]. [Name] is [one sentence summary of who you are and what you are doing to build credibility]. He is highly skilled at [insert what you do] and eager to serve. [Name] will be calling you in the next few weeks.

------END-------

Here are the names you wrote down:
• Name 1

- Name 2
- Name 3
- Name 4
- Name 5
- Name 6

Thank you!
[signature]

After you've sent the email, you can engage with the person who was referred to you. This call template might help. Of course, adapt it to what works best for your unique situation:

Hi, is this Michael? Hey Michael, my name is Dave Brown, and my name might not ring a bell for you because you and I haven't met yet. The reason I'm calling is because you were recommended to me by a mutual friend, Alyssa Hanson.

By chance, did she give you a heads-up that I would be calling? Well, Alyssa had the nicest things to say about you! [If possible, include something you discovered during your Pre-approach. For example, "She told me that you're a huge Titans fan."]

Great! Also, I'm just curious, how did you originally meet Alyssa? [Be quiet and let them tell the story.]

That's cool. Well, Alyssa and I met at _____ [tell your story if you have one].

[Transition by saying . . .] As a matter of fact, I also happen to be Alyssa's ____ [sales coach, financial advisor, Realtor—whatever your professional relationship is]. For the last ten years I've been working with her to [insert your *why*. For example, "lower her tax burden, manage her real estate, hire great staff"].

Anyway, Alyssa mentioned that it would be worth giving you a call to chat for a few minutes. She said that she really values your relationship and thought it would be worth connecting with you to see if I might help you and serve you with [state what you do].

What I'd like to do is get together for thirty minutes to get to know you a little bit and hear about some of your business goals. I'm available on Monday or Wednesday of next week. Which of those days would work better for you? [Close for the appointment.]

These templates are intended to move you forward, and they are proven to work. Make them work for you.

When you complete the Getting Referrals step, you will be light years ahead of most salespeople. Be scripted and strategic by following the techniques in this chapter, and you will be positioned to break through to another level.

Putting the Principles into Action

Create a custom referral script based on the 7-Step Referral Process. Share it with your sales manager or trusted peer to get feedback. Practice it and use it.

To get in the right headspace, create an index card with three affirmations about getting referrals. Here are some affirmations that work for me:

"Since I am dedicated to servant selling, I want to help as many people as I can. Asking for names of potential new clients is important to my mission."

"I am a referral-gathering master. Everyone I speak with gives me a lot of referrals."

"People appreciate how I help them, so they reciprocate by giving me a ton of referrals."

Schedule regular time in your calendar to reengage your existing customer base using the SRE Technique.

Part Three

COMMIT TO SUCCESS AND SERVICE

CHAPTER 13

TAME THE TIME CRUNCH

With More Hours Freed Up, You Have More Hours to Serve

Matt Poliseno is a coaching client I have worked with for five years. When we began working together, he was starting a new company in a new city. He struggled constantly with issues related to procrastination, which led to anxiety and self-blame.

Matt's daily schedule was a mess, and it was strangling his productivity. He hated the roller coaster. He would be on top of his appointments and tasks for a few days, feeling great about getting things done, and then completely fall off the time-management track and go back to his negative place. It took Matt years to grasp that everything starts and stops with his schedule and his choice to abide by it.

In our coaching work, we started small. Together, we listed all the things he would like to get done over the week. We then started plugging those items into a simple spreadsheet he could reference daily to keep on track. At first, he resisted the rigidity of it, saying things like, "I can't plan how things are going to go. So many things come up unexpectedly, and I need to handle them when they do." My colleagues and I often hear this from many of our coaching clients, but we keep reminding them that their schedule is their lifeline.

Servant sellers realize that when they are on schedule, they are moving from task to task in the most efficient way. This allows them to give full attention to whoever they are meeting because they are free of distractions and preoccupations. It was extremely helpful for Matt to understand that when his schedule got off track, it would usually continue to unravel until he was behind in his tasks. When this happened, he became completely reactive rather than proactive.

Now Matt is transformed because of the small but intentional decisions he makes daily. As a result, he has helped many people. He has started eight businesses in five years. Two of them have successfully been sold, four others are productive and profitable, and two others are ramping up and growing. He manages his hectic agenda by planning and then executing what he is going to do. This frees his mind to focus on serving rather than on a chaotic schedule.

Don't Think About It

Why do we tend to go off track? I'm stepping on my soapbox to talk about one of the worst human habits. It is the most negative and unproductive habit I see in salespeople—and I see it all the time. It's probably something you're guilty of doing on a regular basis. I'm guilty too.

Ready for it?

Ladies and gentlemen, you've got to *stop thinking*. I'll say it again. *Stop! Thinking!* Every day, we waste time thinking about tasks, weighing possibilities or outcomes, reviewing results, and fixating on doubts and rejections. It is wasted time that could—and absolutely should—be spent on sales activity.

For example, let's say you hear a no from a prospect. What do you do? If you're like a lot of people, you then spend the next fifteen minutes or more replaying the call, wondering what you could have said or done differently. Before you know it, fifteen minutes have turned into an hour with no productive activity. That time would have been better spent making more calls to help more people.

When you don't have to think about your routine activities, you can reserve your mental capacity for focusing on others. Servant salespeople set up their day so that they can give people their best.

I take this idea so seriously that I've set up my whole life so that I don't have to think—or rather, so that I don't have to think about things that are a waste of time. How? By creating systems, just like Matt learned to do. I schedule what's most important to me so that I don't have to think during the day.

Sales calls? On my selling days, I make forty-two a day. I don't even think about it. Lunch? I subscribe to a premade keto meal delivery service. After two minutes in the microwave, my healthy food is in front of me, or I make a salad that I prepped on the weekend. Fitness? I work out every day at the same time. No exceptions. No decision to make.

I've been using systems to stop thinking as far back as when I was a kid. For instance, I would make my bed in the morning before anybody told me to because it was easier and more comfortable for me to get into bed at night.

When you put systems in place that allow you to operate on autopilot, without having to make a thousand little decisions every day, you unlock the key to successful time management.

You know, of course, that I'm not telling you to *never* think about selling. You should invest the time initially to set your goals, set your direction, figure out what you want to do, and get your system in place. Then you don't have to think about it anymore; you just execute the system.

Is there a time for evaluation, reflection, and strategizing? Yes—just not during the workday, when you should be busy helping and serving others.

All the Time in the World

Scheduling and time management are critically important to success, not just in your sales career but in life. From a servant selling perspective, if you're not managing your time, you're not serving other people well.

This concept is so foundational that our coaches spend their first couple of calls with one-on-one clients focusing on scheduling their optimal week. Our coaches understand that if you don't know what a perfect week looks like, you'll never have one. Sure, you may get thrown off track now and then when emergencies pop up. But as quickly as possible, you'll fall right back into your optimal schedule and move forward with what you're supposed to be doing—with no thinking involved!

When it comes to managing your time, the truth is that you have all the time in the world. How you schedule it determines how much time you can use. How often have you heard people, including yourself, say they don't have enough time? Whenever you admit that you're lacking something, you lose the power to control it. If you say you don't have time, you'll believe there's nothing you can do about it. Then it's easy to get down on yourself. You start hearing yourself say things like you're not getting everything done, you're overwhelmed, or you're spread too thin. When this happens, your emotions have taken over the conversation—and that's not good. When you make these statements, you are also sending a message to other people that they are not a priority. That isn't service.

I'm not saying you're not legitimately busy. I'm saying that you need to stop telling yourself and others you are. I encounter so many people who mess this up daily by saying to themselves or others, "I have so much on my plate" or "I'm so busy" or "How am I going to get to it all?" These people have lost control of their time, and because of that, they have lost much of their quality of life.

That's why if someone says to me, "I know you're busy"—I literally stop them. I say, "I'm not busy. I've got all the time in the world." I've come to hate the word *busy* because we use it as an excuse not to take control of the time we have. The expression "I have all the time in the world" has revitalized my perspective on time and my interactions with people. The next time you feel overwhelmed, stop and say, "I have all the time in the world." After saying it ten times, you'll start feeling differently about time. Once you win the emotional battle, you'll be able to master your time so you can serve more people.

Now when someone asks me for my time, I say, "Of course!" Then I look at my calendars and schedule a meeting. It doesn't matter if it's next week, a month, or even two months away— now it's scheduled. The emotion has been taken out of it.

Say over and over throughout your day, "I have all the time in the world." And watch what happens.

Golden Hours

When we help our coaching clients set up an optimal week schedule, one thing we encourage them to do is to figure out their Golden Hours. These hours are when you are doing income-producing activities (IPAs)—and that's all you're doing. It's a time block when you're dedicated exclusively to creating momentum, working smarter, and being proactive (versus waiting for something to hit your desk).

The concept of Golden Hours comes from creating momentum consistently every day during your times of maximum productivity. So many people squander the opportunity to work smart because they operate their schedule around whenever they feel like prospecting or calling. But if you're thinking like a servant seller, the first key to working the Golden Hours concept is to ask, "When is the best time for my prospect to be reached?" I call on leaders of sales teams, and I have found that the best time to reach them is either first thing in the morning (7:30–9:30 a.m.) or late in their workday (4:00–6:00 p.m.).

Determine your Golden Hours for maximizing your energy and your potential clients' availability. Once you've identified the best time to reach your prospects or recruits, create a system to protect your Golden Hours. First, schedule your Golden Hours in your calendar as if they are the most important times in your day—because they are. Plan them into your schedule each week. If you are doing the same job week in and out, keep your Golden Hours at the same time each day. Don't waste a second of that time. Have your top twenty prospects listed and ready to call. I even suggest you stand during that hour to keep your energy level high. Eliminate all possible distractions. Put a sign on your door that reads something like, "Golden Hours in progress. I'm currently investing valuable time in _____. Please do not interrupt." Whatever it takes!

Pat Roach, the person who recruited me to sell for Southwestern Advantage years ago and is now the president of Southwestern Real Estate, is one of the best leaders I have ever known. He told me that for every minute you are off schedule, it takes two minutes to get back on schedule. This is so true! Turn off any notifications before your Golden Hours. Don't check email, answer questions, take personal calls, or answer any call unless it is from someone setting a new appointment. Make sure you even use the bathroom first. Then dial as many numbers as possible.

Anyone can work intensely for one or two hours every day. By sectioning off Golden Hours in your day, you will be able to get the most important things done while not giving in to what author Charles E. Hummel called the "tyranny of the urgent."

Two Birds, One Stone

Another great time-management concept is the Two Birds, One Stone approach. This is when you combine tasks efficiently and effectively. This synergistic process can be as simple as listening to podcasts, audiobooks, or training recordings while you're driving between appointments or walking the dog. It may involve practicing your sales talk while you're showering. I've even applied this concept to networking by inviting some guys to play a game of basketball, which I enjoy doing more than drinking beers in a bar. I got this idea from one of my coaching clients, Rich Woo at Northwestern Mutual in Chicago. He is a master at bringing people together for fun, fellowship, and fitness. Sometimes he talks business when he is with a group, and sometimes he doesn't. His goal is to bring together like-minded people and facilitate discussions. Rich is networking and connecting people . . . and sometimes getting a good workout in.

With the Two Birds, One Stone technique, you can group your face-to-face visits to minimize travel time. Google Maps has a "Routes" feature that allows you to input up to twenty-five waypoints and calculates the most efficient routes. Utilizing that system eliminates the planning you might otherwise have to do, allowing you to focus on serving others without thinking about where you are going next.

Delegating: The Secret Sauce

One of the biggest needle movers for streamlining and freeing up time is delegating to an assistant. If you're doing work that could be done by someone with less experience, you're wasting precious time. You should be doing the work that only you can do; if someone else can do it for you, it's time to hire an assistant. When you are serious about helping as many people as possible and doing it well, it almost always makes sense to delegate.

Why are we reluctant to delegate? We often think that someone else can't do certain tasks as well as we can. Then, when we finally do hand over those tasks, the assistant messes it up like we thought they would. Delegating is not about perfection, though: it's about progress. I bet the first time you did that same task, you messed it up too. Mistakes will happen, but when you have the right assistant in place the mistakes will be few and the learning process quick.

Most of us are making decisions rooted in an old paradigm of time management; we think our minutes and hours need to be governed by the urgency of today instead of the significance of tomorrow. I call this Significance Thinking.

Are you emailing back and forth multiple times to schedule a meeting? Entering or updating data in your client resource management software? Handling the same simple customer questions over and over? Creating spreadsheets or PowerPoints?

Looking up information about a new prospect? All of this could be easily managed by a good assistant, either virtual or in-office.

This solution to time management usually comes with some pushback from our coaching clients. They are hesitant to hire someone because they don't want to spend the money. They see it as an expense they can't afford and are worried about the time it would take to train a person to do the work well. This situation needs to be reframed toward Significance Thinking. In reality, you multiply your time when you delegate to an assistant, making it more than worth the additional investment.

The world's most effective managers adopt Significance Thinking by applying the 30x Rule. This classic sales rule says you should spend 30x the amount of time training someone to do a task as it would take you to do the task yourself once. For example, if a task takes you five minutes per day to complete, then the 30x rule suggests you could spend up to 150 minutes training someone to do that task.

Most managers think it's crazy to spend two-and-a-half hours training someone to do a five-minute task. They tell themselves, "It would just be faster to do it myself." That's because most managers are stuck in classic "urgency" thinking—they are only evaluating their tasks inside the construct of one day. With those parameters, it never makes sense to spend two-and-a-half hours to train someone on a task that they could do in five minutes.

But Significance Thinkers know that any task that takes you five minutes a day for 250 working days in a year comes out to 1,250 total minutes. Investing 150 minutes (30 x 5) into training someone to do a task that takes five minutes a day is still a highly effective use of time. If you divide 150 minutes (the time you spent training) into 1,100 (the net amount of time it saves you over the course of a year after you deduct the time you spent training) that yields a 733 percent ROTI (Return on Time Invested).

Grant yourself permission to accept temporary imperfection. Invest time into delegating today so you can create more time tomorrow, which will help you to serve your prospects more effectively.

Hiring an assistant is a big commitment, but over the years, I've heard feedback from hundreds of coaching clients that having an assistant has helped them make the most of their time. Mark Cleve, who works for Tom James, a custom clothing company, was a Southwestern Consulting client for six years. In that time, Mark rose through the ranks, starting as an office leader to become the division vice president. Mark credits his assistant with much of his success, saying, "I hired an amazing assistant who is excellent. He loves the business and loves to learn. I am free to focus on what I am supposed to be focused on—growing my business. As a result, at the end of this month, I will have had my best rolling twelve months ever in my twenty-one-year career."

Another client, L. V. Granger, owns a holding company in Columbia, South Carolina. He notes that adding an assistant onto his team has allowed him to spend more focused time with his family and has made his life less stressful: "Even while hiring an assistant, my increase in production has allowed me to realize a net increase in my income by 40 percent!"

Max Harbuck, principal of Lakeshore Benefit Alliance in Birmingham, Alabama, does employee benefit consulting. He hired an assistant and has seen significant results. "In the past, my activity was very sporadic," he explains. "There was no consistency at all. My prospecting was done in spurts and, therefore, my business came in spurts as well. Now I've created the habit of dialing every day and utilizing my assistant much more. The results are obvious. My production has increased by 33 percent and my income by 23 percent!"

These are just a few examples of clients who have benefitted from having an assistant. When you invest in an assistant to help you make the most of your time, you'll be revitalized and better able to focus on what matters most: serving your customers.

Putting the Principles into Action

Plan your optimal week. Decide when your Golden Hours need to be scheduled each week and plug those times in first. Then plan your meetings and appointments around this protected time.

Conduct a Systems Audit. Analyze your daily routine and determine where you might put systems in place to eliminate the need to think. Where in your schedule can you make decisions around that routine or task?

Conduct a Delegation Audit. Take a close look at how you spend your time each day. Note which tasks could be handed off to an assistant. Pay attention to how much time you spend on each task. Imagine having that additional time in your schedule to reach more people!

CHAPTER 14

SET GOALS TO SERVE BETTER

Reverse Engineer Your Way to Success

If you've ever run a marathon, half-marathon, or even a 5K, you know how encouraging it is to see the distance you've traveled marked on signposts along the way. It's concrete evidence of your progress. Goals function in the same way, showing your momentum toward the finish line. Setting goals is essential to becoming the person you envision for yourself. When you set goals, you're seeing yourself as the person you want to be, rather than seeing yourself for who you are right now.

Many people think about goal setting in terms of numbers, but servant salespeople think beyond the numbers. They set their goals strategically, thinking about how they will help their prospects and clients. They also think beyond work goals, focusing on personal development.

As a servant seller, I want to make sure that I'm giving my best self to everyone from my coworkers to my clients to my children and Emmie. Improving my personal relationships helps my working relationships. For example, if I get better at saying sorry to my wife and kids, I'll get better at apologizing to my clients. Saying "I'm sorry" seems basic, but those simple words help me develop an awareness that the other person is not having their needs met. This is an important skill that will enable me to better serve my clients, family, and friends by reading them well and showing empathy.

Goal setting can seem overwhelming. I always tell people that when you're setting goals, you need to think about words ending in "ally" that are important to you: the areas you want to grow spiritually, physically, emotionally, professionally, and financially. You should examine each aspect of your life and set goals around it. Ask yourself, "If everything worked out perfectly in this area in the coming year, what would that look like?" Dream big and tie your goals to concrete steps.

The goal-setting process always comes back to action steps. For example, if I want to grow relationally, I might set these goals:

"This year, I will spend quality, extended time with my two best friends."

How much time exactly?

"Four guy trips this year would be good, at least a weekend each and longer if we can arrange it."

I set a goal to email my friends and settle on dates. Then I set another goal to book the locations by the end of next week. That's just one example of how I might take a bigger vision (quality time with my two best friends throughout the year) and reverse engineer it into concrete action steps to make it happen.

Dream Big about Your Big Picture

Every five years or so, I set big goals, which I compile into a list of twenty-five to thirty affirmations that I keep on me at all times, in the Notes app on my phone. Over the years, whenever I have powerful thoughts of who I want to be, I make notes in my phone. When I'm inspired at church or at a conference or by a conversation, I add to that note. I also send text messages to myself about ways I want to improve my marriage, parenting, career, and so on.

I spend ten to twelve hours gathering my ideas in early January. Then I organize my thoughts into collections, ending up with twenty-five to thirty batches of inspirational quotes and ideas. Next comes the hard part—editing and focusing the ideas to specifically support my goals. I edit each batch down, synthesizing it into one or two sentences in a standard Word document.

This process takes focused time. Sometimes I'll spend two hours on one batch to make the sentence concise and sharp. When my sentences are completed, I'll take another five to six hours to add internal codes that motivate me each time I read my goals. This keeps me engaged.

I like to phrase goals using affirmations or assurances that these ambitions will take place. I don't want to say, "I hope to ..." or "I want to ..." That seems speculative and uncertain. Instead, my goals are phrased as "I am doing this ..." or "I do this ..." I encourage my coaching clients to write their goals this way. My client Jon Milonas said, "Setting my goals in affirmation form has been the most important thing I have done to keep a positive mental framework in every area of my life."

My five-year goals often include twenty-five or thirty affirmations, but I'll keep things simple and provide twelve examples here. Note that some of the words on this list are intentionally misspelled. The list also includes specific stylistic elements and characters. These codes are unique to me. You might come up with your own that have meaning to you.

The first code is using standard double quotation marks for disciplines that I am constantly working on—phrases and ideas that are major sources of transformation for me. These quoted words are my compass for how I want to live my life in service to others.

The second code involves using single quotation marks. These are my big hits—important things I need to focus on and improve. I emphasize them with single quotation marks as a reminder that I need to be working on them daily.

The third code is intentionally misspelling words I don't like. For instance, you'll probably notice below that the word *lose* is misspelled as *loose*. I hate the word so much that I have even misspelled it twice! I do this because I hate losing, and I don't want to give the word any respect or credit.

These codes are my idiosyncrasies—little tricks I use to highlight some words or diminish others as I strive to serve others. You might try this when creating your own goal affirmations.

Here are some of my personal and work-related goals:

- I do & talk about hard things to be an example to others to do & speak about "hard things" in their lives.
- I keep my cool and don't react poorly with my kids and wife. I am 'empathetic & kind' to them all the time.
- Emmie & I are forever connected. I am quick to say "I'm sorry" & work to show her she is most important to me.
- I exercise & build physical & mental muscles daily. I make good eating choices & take care of my body.
- I am a servant to all, especially with my family. I always look for ways to serve & help everyone around me, daily.

- I use my competitive nature to bring joy to the world & loose graciously. I think & say, 'good game' when I loose.
- I work to increase my "gratefulness quotient" weekly. When I'm grateful, I'm humble. I am grateful for what I have.
- I think & act strategically to move our company forward every year & I 'share the credit' with my partners.
- I make time for everything that is important in my life; "I have all the time in the world." Especially for Emmie & our kids.
- I "excel-orate" people daily. I see beauty & goodness all around me, especially in the people I interact & do life with.
- I lead, create & produce generational leaders. It's one of my most valuable traits. I am a Level 100 Leader.
- I am a master delegator. I fully trust the people in my life that support me. Progress is my focus & then perfection.

Refine Your Goal-Setting Skills

Setting goals may seem like common sense, but as the saying goes, common sense is not always common practice. Here are some specific tips we use to help top performers refine their goal-setting skills:

1. Write down your goals. Writing your goals on paper takes them out of your head and puts them somewhere concrete. This is the first step to achieving your goals. Research strongly favors systematically writing and tracking your goals. Why? You're more likely to remember and focus on anything that you've written down.

It's such a simple step that it's hard to argue against buying a planner or having a notebook dedicated to your goals!

2. Make your goals SMART. This well-known acronym was first credited to consultant George Doran in 1981. I have included it here because it works for me and will for you too.

Specific: "I will be one of the top five service-oriented sellers in our company by the end of this year" versus "I will help more people this year."

Measurable: "I will get twenty-five *no* responses every day before I finish my workday" versus "I will make more calls each day."

Attainable: "I will increase my sales revenue by 15 percent over the next six months" versus "I will 10x my sales revenue by the end of the month."

Relevant: "I will secure a top servant-selling coach for our team before the end of the month" versus "I'd like my sales-people to talk to a professional who can help them with their taxes."

Time-Frame: "I will meet with ten new clients each month" versus "I will increase my meetings with new clients."

3. Connect emotionally with your goals: Meaningless goals often come from people who were forced to participate in goal-setting sessions at their businesses or with their spouses or friends. A goal should move you emotionally and inspire action. If your goals are generic, empty, and void of emotion, then they are unlikely to be accomplished because they don't mean anything to you.

4. Break down your goals into milestones. You've identified the finish line, so what do the mile markers along the way look like? Maybe you want to set a personal goal to listen during 90 percent of your sales conversations over the next week so you can better serve others. Or maybe you want to earn the

Founder's Club distinction and win a trip to Fiji. What needs to happen first? Brainstorm a list of everything you can think of that would need to happen to reach your goals, and then . . .

5. Identify the first step. What is the first step you can take today toward that mile marker? Do it!

6. Visualize. Envision what it will look like after you achieve your goals. How will you feel? Who will be with you? What will you do after you hit your goals?

If you've created a vision board and identified your goals by writing them as affirmations, the visualization process should be easy. Envisioning the outcome simply brings to life what you have written down or placed on a board.

7. Share your goals. Find positive people—like a coach, mentor, or accountability partner—who will encourage you and keep you accountable. Do not share your goals with people who will not help you or support you in achieving them. For example, if you strive to be a service-oriented salesperson, then avoid mentors and coaches who only prioritize making money and don't understand your desire to help people.

8. Unconditionally commit. Quitting is not an option. Reaching your goals might take five to ten years, or it might take only one year. Either way, never lose sight of your dream.

These eight steps will help you reverse engineer your way to success. Becoming clear on your goals and having a focused plan to accomplish them will put you into a highly productive state, empowering you to make steady progress. When you are achieving your servant selling goals, everyone you speak with will get the best "you."

Continuous Review on the Journey

Setting goals is not a one-and-done proposition. All goals need to be reviewed regularly: short-term goals should be assessed on a weekly basis, mid-term goals on a monthly or quarterly basis, and long-term goals at least annually.

Schedule time accordingly and make an appointment on your calendar to take this critical step to success. Many people I coach find Sunday evenings to be a great time to review their short-term goals and make plans for the week ahead. Whatever time you schedule, be sure to review each goal and include all forward progress, even if it seems small.

Next, list any roadblocks, followed by solutions. If you do not know what is holding you back, decide where or how you will find the answer and then pursue it. This is one of the areas where having a great coach can help you break through.

If you have achieved your goals, increase them. If you did not achieve your goals, adjust your time frame and create an action plan for how to get there.

If you are on pace with your activity goals but not seeing the results you want, review your numbers to see which area you need to improve in and map out a plan for improvement. For example, if you are making lots of calls and not setting many appointments, decide this week to study your phone script and work on your Pre-approach and Approach. Figure out what's keeping you from setting appointments with people you want to help.

Once you've dedicated the time to setting your goals, put them where you can see them. (My own goals are posted all over my house!) Then invite the people closest to you—whether it's your team, spouse, family, close friends, or whoever—to write their own goals. Place their goals where you can see them. This way, you're not only looking at your own goals, you're also looking at the goals of people closest to you and letting their goals inspire you.

If you walked into my office, you would see the goals posted for each person I directly manage and the goals for other people who are important to me. These goals are printed out, slipped into a page protector with each person's name at the top, and taped to my wall. I ask for their updated goals each year.

It pumps me up to look at the individuals my team members and loved ones are going to become. I get excited to think about their growth. Sometimes I know their goals better than they do because I see them all the time on my walls. It gives them an accountability partner who cares about them and what they want to accomplish. It gives them somebody who will ask them about their progress. It gives me accountability to stay attuned to my own goals.

What's more, keeping others' goals posted in my office shows the people in my life that I value them. It shows what they want to accomplish, which then becomes important to me. It reminds me that I am helping my friends, family, and team members reach their goals. Anybody on my team who walks into my office will feel important.

When you invest the time and effort to become clear on where you're going and then engage in the goal-setting process on a regular basis, you will be able to serve more people.

Putting the Principles into Action

Write out every word ending in "ally" that represents areas of life that are important to you (such as financially, spiritually, relationally, emotionally, or physically). Then set goals around each of these words. Servant sellers might choose different words than a traditional salesperson would. Be creative.

What specific goals do you have as a servant seller? Write them down in affirmation form. Then hang up the page somewhere in your house or office where you will see it every day.

Name your most important goal. Begin the process to reverse engineer this goal by identifying daily and weekly activities you can do to ensure you hit each one of them.

CHAPTER 15

ACCENTUATE ACCOUNTABILITY

Enlist Others to Help You Sell and Serve More Effectively

It is impossible to imagine a successful businessperson who lacks accountability. It is also impossible to imagine an effective servant salesperson who lacks accountability.

To be accountable means to live with integrity—when all your thoughts, words, and actions are consistent with one another and align with your overarching vision. Sure, you may say you're committed to helping people and believe wholeheartedly that you are. But while commitment is part of being a successful servant seller, accountability is the key to sustaining long-term success.

As I mentioned previously, in the early days of Southwestern Consulting, we held large, professional sales training conferences all over the country. We sold tens of thousands of tickets to people who came to learn sales and leadership techniques from us. When we surveyed our participants at the end of each event, we received many comments asking for guidance in taking the next step. One person wrote, "This was the best seminar I have ever attended. Now who's going to help me integrate all these techniques into my life? Do you all do that?" Another attendee told us, "You guys hit a home run. My entire office is going back to work tomorrow with a fire lit under them. Thank you! What's next? Do you have a follow-up program? I don't want this one to wear off like others have in the past." These are actual answers to survey questions from our first couple of conferences.

After getting several requests for coaching services and many more requests recognizing the need for a mentor to stay on track, we decided to create a coaching program in 2008 that offers professional accountability. This was one of the best decisions we've ever made for the company, and we have now coached tens of thousands of people one-on-one.

Finding an Accountability Relationship

Since launching our coaching program, we have learned that people who want to be successful understand the need for accountability and seek it out so they can keep moving toward success.

There are different levels of accountability, from meeting with friends to joining support groups to hiring a professional coach. At the very least, you need a neutral accountability partner who connects with you at regular intervals. This could be a friend, mentor, coach, or trusted colleague—ideally someone who has more experience than you. This might be someone you know well, or it might be a coach you recently hired. Whatever the case, you must be able to openly share your struggles, setbacks, and successes. Most of all, this person must be able and willing to hold you accountable to the things that are important to you.

Some people prefer to use accountability by joining a support group where they talk through their issues and find solutions to their problems. They report their progress to the group, but they also support the other members by holding them accountable.

There is value in seeing accountability from both sides, and group accountability can be helpful, but I believe it is not as effective as meeting with someone individually. When someone is working with you on exactly what you are trying to accomplish and then is consistently holding you accountable, that's where the magic happens.

My good friend and business partner Bruce Pommier used a great metaphor to describe the accountability process to me:

Imagine you are in Nashville with your phone in your hand and you want to get to Miami. When you open a GPS app on your phone and type in "Miami," your GPS analyzes where you are standing right now and gives you a few route options. You naturally want to pick the fastest route.

From there, the GPS maps out your trip and gives you turn-by-turn directions to Miami. You know it's going to be a long trip. You also know there is going to be traffic, accidents, road construction, weather, and pit stops along the way. Delays and detours will happen. Still, the job of the GPS is to keep you on track and headed in the fastest direction.

Having a coach or accountability partner is the same thing. Whatever goal or dream you have is your Miami. It is the coach's job to keep you on track, knowing that you are going to run into all sorts of obstacles. Having an accountability coach keeps you on the fastest route to your goal. Your coach is the GPS voice telling you to get off at the next exit or to get back on the inter-state as soon as possible.

That metaphor is exactly right. I believe in coaching so much that I have four one-on-one coaches who help me in different areas of my life at various intervals throughout the year: a life and leadership coach (once a month), a tax strate-gist and wealth coach (once a quarter), a marriage coach (once a month), and a parenting coach (once a month). They are my GPS when I'm off course and need help getting back on track.

The Four Requirements of Accountability

In his speech "The Common Denominator of Success," Albert Gray said, "Any resolution or decision you make today has to be made again tomorrow, and the next day, and the next, and the next, and so on."[10] That's why accountability is so important. When you have accountability in your life, you have someone who constantly checks in with you and asks, "Did you do it? Did you do it? Did you do it?" That is so powerful!

For instance, having a personal trainer works so well because, when we don't feel like going to the gym, we're not going to go. But if we pay $50 per session up front, then we'll go even when we don't feel like it!

There are four "musts" for a good accountability system:

1. There must be pain or cost associated with inaction.
   With your accountability partner or group, decide on a conse-quence for inaction and make it hurt. What is the point of having an accountability partner who lets you off the hook and says, "You didn't follow through? Oh well. No biggie. Try to do better next time." That response may be kind and understanding, but it's not accountability.

For accountability to be effective, there must be some penalty or loss when you don't meet standards that you agreed upon. Wise parents understand this principle well and tell their kids, "You didn't do your chores this week— the chores you agreed to—so you won't be getting your allowance."

2. There must be 360-degree accountability.

The people holding you accountable should include a subordinate or mentee who looks up to you, a spouse or colleague who is your equal, and an objective third party who you employ (such as a coach or trainer). Each of these people will have a different influence over you, which will help you take action.

3. Accountability must be regular and reliable.

You can't check in once in a while and get the best results. Accountability should be part of a regular schedule that you determine ahead of time with your partner(s). Consistency is key.

4. Accountability must come from someone who can give perspective.

Seek out accountability from others who have been there, done that—or done something significant like what you are working toward. Be skeptical of accountability partners who are not also top performers. Don't forget the old saying: "You can't teach what you don't know. And you can't lead where you don't go."

Remember that in all areas of life, the cost of accountability is always much cheaper than the cost of inaction.

Extra Accountability

If it were easy to achieve our biggest goals, and every step along the way was fun and exciting, we would have little need for accountability. But that's just not how it works in the real world. When we find ourselves facing things we don't want to do, it's important to acknowledge those things and then take action.

People are often scared of what's on the other side of accountability because they don't want to do things that push them out of their comfort zone. Albert Einstein is often credited with saying, "We cannot solve our problems with the same thinking we used when we created them." If you want a different result, you need to integrate someone or something else into the process. That's where extra accountability comes into play. It's like an insurance policy.

Away Motivation

Here's an example of how away motivation works. I have mentioned one of my coaching clients, Jon Milonas, who is a senior vice president with CBRE in Chicago. On one of our coaching calls, we figured out that he needed to have ten Golden Hours and eighty touches (emails, calls, texts) for two weeks to meet a particular goal. We decided to add extra accountability to raise the stakes for him on keeping his Golden Hours.

"Who annoys you in your industry?" I asked him. "Maybe not in your office, but who just really gets under your skin?"

"Oh, I definitely know," Jon replied. "I used to work with this guy I'll call 'Jerry,' and we were really competitive and still are to some extent."

"Okay, got it. If you don't meet your Golden Hours challenge, you have to send Jerry a check for $1,000 and say, 'Thank you for everything you've taught me about this industry.'"

"Oh, no!" Jon immediately responded. "That is *never* going to happen. Yes, let's add this extra accountability because I am *not* going to let that happen. Ever!"

This added incentive, or inspiration, worked for Jon, and we have continued to put extra accountability measures in place over the last five years. This is called *away* motivation because it is moving away from something you don't want.

Toward Motivation

My good friend and fellow coach Steve Reiner uses *toward* motivation. One year, he promised his daughter Anika that if he sold fifty coaching clients in a specific campaign (a six-month period), they would see the Broadway hit musical *Hamilton* in New York City. (At the time, tickets started at about the typical cost of a car payment, and the best seats were priced higher than some mortgage payments!)

Anika had always wanted to see *Hamilton*, so she asked Steve every day, "Did you make your calls today? Did you do the deal today, Dad?" Every day. She literally came to his home office every day for six months at 5:30 p.m. to check up on him. He met his goal. And they went to see *Hamilton*.

Extra accountability works. How do you know if you respond better to *away* or *toward* motivation? Test it. Try it one way and see if it works well for you. If not, try the other. In either case, be sure that the stakes are extremely high.

Critical Success Factors

Another way to hold yourself accountable is by tracking what Southwestern Consulting calls Critical Success Factors (CSFs), also known as Key Performance Indicators (KPIs). This is an internal system for achieving your big goals by reverse engineering them way down to their smallest steps and then executing on those.

You can break down your annual goal into what you need to achieve quarterly, monthly, weekly, and even daily. When you track your progress each day and realize you are starting to veer off course, you can correct yourself much more easily than if you wait until the end of the month, the quarter, or the year. When you combine this technique with accountability to hit your CSFs, you have the potential to succeed at a level you've only dreamed of achieving. Servant salespeople learn to love accountability by tracking their CSFs because it works. By following this accountability system, they can help their prospects and clients to the best of their ability.

Here is a concrete example of how to reverse engineer your sales goals around a performance target to achieve your maximum earning and serving potential. Suppose you are in a commission sales environment. You may want to scribble some numbers on a sheet of paper as you go:

1. Define your Yearly Performance Target.
2. Then jot down your Average Commission Per Sale.
3. Find your Yearly Customer Goal. To do that, divide your yearly performance target (#1) by your average commission per sale (#2).
4. Set your Monthly Customer Goal. Divide your yearly customer goal (#3) by the number of months you work in a year.
5. Then find your Weekly Customer Goal by dividing your monthly customer goal (#4) by four.
6. Compute your Weekly Appointment Goal. Divide your weekly customer goal (#5) by your average closing percentage. How many of those appointments do you typically end up closing? Be realistic here.

7. Find your Daily Call Goal. Just divide your daily appointment goal (#6) by your appointment-setting ratio.

To get even more structured, you can divide your daily call goal by four two-hour segments called Goal Periods. If you do those segments four times a day for the same average number of days per week you usually work, for the same average number of weeks per year you usually work, you will hit your goals.

Notice how this entire system is focused on activity and not on results. The results always come by doing your CSF activity. The students in the training program at Southwestern Advantage have one focus. It's not how much money they're going to make. Of course, that is part of the draw for them, but we put the most emphasis on executing the CSFs. We say, "You want to be successful? Show your programs to thirty families a day. Just show the programs to thirty families a day. That's it. And you will win at this job."

Given that Southwestern has been doing this for over 165 years and is still going strong, I'd say the system has proven itself. (I can personally attest that it works!) Focus on the activity level you need to engage in to meet your goals rather than the results you want to achieve. Mix that with accountability to keep yourself focused and on track, and amazing things will happen to you as a servant seller.

One Last Word

The longer I live and the more personal development work I do on myself and with others, the more convinced I am that accountability is the secret ingredient to success, peace, fulfillment, and joy. Actually, it is the not-so-secret ingredient, because most people know accountability is necessary for success—they just don't want to do it.

To be honest, I don't like being held accountable, but it works every time I add it to another area of my life. It's not the path of least resistance; this path is usually filled with tough conversations and early morning workouts and uncomfortable situations. That is exactly why it is so effective.

Accountability means that you'll be doing hard things, but when you have accountability, life will get easier. As humans we are not meant to go through life alone. If you are great at holding yourself accountable, that's good. You should be proud. I'm not very good at being accountable on my own. I believe we were all created for camaraderie, and accountability ensures we grow with and because of others' help.

It's fitting that this is the last chapter of my book because the man I am today is a result of the people who have cared enough about me to hold me accountable to do what I need to do—especially when I don't feel like it. (Remember WYDFLI from chapter 4?) Take a minute to think about all the people in your life who hold you accountable and push you to work toward becoming the person you want to be. You probably feel an overwhelming sense of gratitude for them right now, like I feel for the accountability-keepers in my life.

Accountability will allow you to do a better job helping everyone you meet through the products and services you offer. If you don't have true accountability in your life, find a coach, trainer, therapist, group, colleague, or good friend to help you. If you already have some accountability in your life, add some extra layers of it so you can serve more people.

Putting the Principles into Action

- Conduct an accountability audit of your habits. Make a list of the major areas where you seem to let yourself down the most in life.

- Apply the four requirements of accountability to each of these major areas in which you are not doing well. To reiterate, the four requirements of accountability are:

  » There must be pain or cost associated with inaction.
  » There must be 360-degree accountability.
  » Accountability must be regular and reliable.
  » Accountability must come from someone who can give perspective.

- Focus specifically on the second requirement: 360-degree accountability with someone behind you, someone next to you, and someone ahead of you. What people in your life fit these criteria? Who can you to ask to hold you accountable?
- Do you respond better to *toward* motivation or *away* motivation? Once identified, apply this type of motivation to a goal you need help achieving.

SERVANT SELLERS NEVER STOP LEARNING AND GROWING

One of the toughest phone calls I have made in a long time occurred just the other day. As I wrote page after page of this book, it became increasingly clear what I needed to do. After a little online research, I tracked down the cell phone numbers for Brian and Beverly Indermuhle. Yes, that couple—the ones I told you about in the introduction to this book. My interaction with that family when I was young and a rookie salesperson, prompted a servant-selling epiphany for me and changed my entire perspective and approach.

I was nervous as I prepared to call Brian and Beverly. All those years ago, I had felt awkward and ashamed for how I had acted in their loving home—I had been self-centered and slightly manipulative as I tried to make a sale. I had not blatantly lied to them, but I had exaggerated and shaded the truth to get the sale. I felt terrible about myself because of it.

Two decades later, what would they say? Would they even take my call? Would they confront me about how I had behaved? I felt so many emotions: anxiousness, apprehension, and awkwardness.

Then, that voice in my head showed up to kill my spirit, steal my joy, and bring on self-doubt. That voice did all it could to talk me out of making the call. It said, "There's no need to make this call. This family forgot about you years ago. It's a noble thing you were going to do here, but that was who you were then and not who you are now. Just let it go, Dave."

I almost did. But I try to push myself to do hard things, so I dialed the number and listened to it ring as my heart pounded. I got a voice mail on the first try and left a jumbled message, not even knowing if the number was a correct one. Then I called the next number feeling a little more confident because I had just conquered some of my initial fear.

"Hello," I heard from the other end. I said my name and asked if I was speaking to Brian Indermuhle, which the person confirmed. I briefly reminded Brian of our sales interaction years ago and the products I sold them. He thought for a moment and then said that yes, he remembered. I explained that I was writing a book on a concept I call servant selling and asked if we could arrange a video chat for that evening.

Five hours later, I found myself looking on-screen at Brian and Beverly, who were sitting at the same kitchen table where we met before—and where I felt sleazy about my sales presentation. They greeted me warmly and we reminisced for a minute. Nervously, I started thanking them for taking the time and asked if I could read them the beginning pages of this book, where I tell their story. I told them they had unknowingly been a major part of my transformation as a sales professional.

I teared up when I read the hard parts of the story to them. When I was done, I said, "I'm sorry. I'm sorry for being that person in your amazing house with your amazing family. I'm sorry that at that point in my life I did not have the integrity to show you the honor and honesty you deserved."

Beverly immediately responded, "Oh, Dave, it's all right. I knew that you had used our sale to get more sales from our neighbors, and that's okay. We love helping people. I'm glad we helped you regardless of what you did and how you felt about it." Then she said, "We forgive you. We forgive you for all of it."

A huge smile appeared on my face, and tears fell from my eyes. I felt so much relief and gratitude for these two people looking at me across many miles.

Beverly went on to talk about how important forgiveness is to their family. Brian and Beverly told me that they taught their four girls that when you wrong someone, you need to sincerely apologize and ask for forgiveness. Beverly said they instilled this principle so deeply into the lives of their daughters—now grown and some with families of their own—that their daughters always try to be people of honesty, humility, and forgiveness.

We talked for the next thirty minutes about all sorts of things, sharing how our lives had evolved, with many joys and struggles along the way. For Brian and Beverly, their devout faith in God had sustained them through it all. I had the strong sense that their home is a place of healing, and they are people of high integrity.

After getting to know the Indermuhles better and realizing we shared a strong Christian faith, I was not surprised that this was the house God chose to teach me powerful lessons of how to sell the honorable way. As we closed our conversation, Beverly extended an invitation to Emmie and me and our kids to someday join them for one of their weekly family suppers, a tradition that has been going on for years. Every Thursday, all their girls and their families come back to the family home for conversation, laughter, and mutual support. I told her to count us in someday. I can't wait for my kids and wife to experience this loving place that transformed me so many years ago!

Transforming Sales

Four days after our call, Brian asked if we could talk again. When we spoke, he shared a story of a young salesperson at his heavy-machinery rental company. The young man was pushing the boundaries of integrity with one of his customers, edging close to the line of dishonesty and manipulation (just as I had years ago). Brian told him about the servant selling philosophy I had shared, and the salesperson chose to take the high road, serving with dignity and honesty. I was thrilled to hear this young man's story. The servanthood approach was already helping transform the sales population for the better! This is my ultimate vision for servant selling.

Sales is such a beautiful profession that many people have done the wrong way for so long. Join me in transforming the way sales transactions happen and changing the way people view salespeople. When you choose to live out the servant selling principles by helping others, it will change your life for the better!

ACKNOWLEDGMENTS

Thank you, Emmie, for interrupting my selfish ways and being the best thing that has ever happened to me. I love you and will work at being connected with you now and forever! Thank you, Dawson, for your unconditional love even though I am as hard on you as I am on myself; I'm forever working on this. Thank you, Cadence, for expanding my heart's capacity to love; you are such a blessing to me and your mom. Thank you, Dylan, for being so cool and calm in the craziness of our lives; you make us so happy and are a great example to all of us.

Thank you to the extended "Brown" family. Bobby and Kristina, I hope you know the impact your abundant love and generosity have on this world. You both teach me so much year after year. Alycia and Zach, you are such amazing people who make everyone around you better, including me. I love and respect you both. Nathan, you are the best audience a brother could ever ask for; I love how much we laugh together. Ben Evers, you are a Brown and my brother; your loyalty and friendship mean more to me than you will ever know. So much of who

I am and will become is because of you and your influence. Love you, Caroline, and the girls! To my other Brown brother from another mother. Together we are literally an "unstoppable force." The way we sharpen one another daily is so special to me. I wouldn't have these servant selling skills or this book if it wasn't for you and your amazing wife. And lastly Henry Bedford, your mentorship and friendship mean the world to me—you're my other dad. Every bit of what we have and will accomplish with Southwestern Consulting is because of you and your guidance. I am forever grateful for all the time you continue to give me. I love you, Barb, and the family more than anything.

Thank you Invictus organization: Adam, Linsmeyer, Merkel, Will, Gena, Bob, Teej, Peter, Christina, Matt, Andrus, Chad, Aaron, and Sarunas. You give Emmie and me purpose, so much joy, and a work family whom we love deeply. Our success wouldn't have happened without you. Words cannot express how grateful we are for you. To all the present SWC coaches and the many to come, I pray this book brings more eyes to this amazing company we get to build together. Ron Alford, thank you for being the best and easiest person to work alongside. We are better together! Sara Hodges, thank you for your trust and friendship. You're so good at everything and so fun! Karen Bannister, I hope you know how much of a blessing you are to Emmie and me; I hope we work and do life together forever. Pat Roach, my entire life changed for the better the day I met you. Please keep recruiting others to our amazing businesses just as you did me; I love and appreciate you so much.

To the entire Southwestern Family of Companies, thank you for valuing people over profits. The way we do business is not normal. I love being a part of something that stands for *what* is right over *who* is right, every time. Cindy Johnstone, your mentorship has been invaluable to me; thank you for it alongside your friendship. Thank you SWFC leaders for leading by example and growing each of your businesses bigger and bigger to serve the world in several different ways. We are all connected through this philosophy of Servant Selling; let's live it out and continue to build! And to the entire Servant Selling team, thank you: Christina, Bill, Keith, AnnJanette, Tim, Chris, KC, Betsy, Hannah, Matt, Mandy, Justin, Jennifer, Lauren, Landry, Landon, and Jonathan. I appreciate all the help.

Thank you, Southwestern Advantage, for being the best place on earth for young people to learn the skills and character they need to be successful in life. There is a reason this business is already over 168 years old and stronger than ever. To all the district sales managers now and forthcoming, your job is the most important one on the planet. Here's to the millions more students whom you will help and serve over the next 168 years. If you are a college student and you are reading this, go online, learn about this internship, and sign up to do it. You'll thank me later.

Thank you, Larry and Donna Romine, Elder Greg Jackson, Pastor Charles Flowers, Kenny and Tina Hope, Aunt Donna, Solomon and Aaron Pendleton, Dennis Arensen, Lance Schrader, Patrick Gilliam, Peter Ferre, Uncle Jimmy, Aunt Barbara, and David Robinson. Each of you had such an impact on my life, and I wouldn't be who I am without your influence. Love you all!

Lastly, to all our past, present, and future clients who sign up for our coaching and training services at Southwestern Consulting (past clients too): without you, we wouldn't have people to be able to practice and live out these Servant Selling principles. You are worth it, and we are honored to participate in your transformation.

Jesus, thank you for always being there for me. You are my Lord and my Savior, and I give this book to you. Your will be done. Love you.

NOTES

1   HubSpot Global Jobs Poll Q2 2016. https://ir.hubspot.com/news/hubspot-reports-q2-2016-results.

2   US Bureau of Labor Statistics, Occupational Employment and Wages, May 2021. https://www.bls.gov/oes/current/oes_nat.htm.

3   The Bridge Group, 2018 SDR Metrics & Compensation Report. https://blog.bridgegroupinc.com/2018-sdr-metrics-report.

4   The Bridge Group, 2015 SaaS Inside Sales Survey Report. https://www.forentrepreneurs.com/bridge-group-2015.

5   CSO Insights, the Research Division of Miller Heiman Group, Fifth Annual Sales Enablement Study, 2019 Sales Enablement Report, pg 8. https://f.hubspotusercontent40.net/hubfs/20881396/CSO-Insights-5th-Annual-Sales-Enablement-Study%20(1).pdf.

6   Salesforce, Third Annual "State of Sales" Report, 2019.

7   Frank Bettger, *How I Raised Myself from Failure to Success in Selling* New York: Cornerstone Library, 1992.

8   "Visualizing Goals Influences Financial Health and Happiness, Study Finds." TD Stories. 20 January 2016. https://stories.td.com/us/en/article/visualizing-goals-influences-financial-health-and-happiness-study-finds.

9   Steve Reiner, *Navigate 2.0: Selling the Way People Like to Buy.* Nashville: Southwestern Consulting, 2016; I recommend this book if you want to figure out how to discover whether your prospect is a Fighter, Entertainer, Detective, or Counselor.

10 This legendary speech was given by Albert Gray in 1940 at the National Association of Life Underwriters (NALU). Gray was an executive with the Prudential Insurance Company of American Agents. The full speech can be found at www.leadershipnow.com/GraySuccess.html.

WANT TO TAKE YOUR SERVANT-SELLING SKILLS TO THE NEXT LEVEL?

Ever wish you could have a coach like Dave in your corner? The world of sales can be tough, and even the best need a little help from time to time!

Get a free consultation from a sales and leadership coach on Dave's team, Southwestern Consulting. We'll help understand your current situation, including your goals, unique obstacles and long-term vision. What is the cost of standing still? What are the unique goals you want to reach? Our professional coaches can help outline a plan to get you from where you are to where you want to be.

HOW DOES COACHING WORK?

Our 12-month Southwestern Coaching program provides tools, resources, and training as part of our proven coaching curriculum to help deliver measurable success over time. In addition, individuals are paired with a coach who helps outline their goals and provide accountability through 1:1 calls each month.

GET A FREE CONSULTATION!